MUSHROOMS

First published in the United States in 1999 by Periplus Editions (HK) Ltd.,
with editorial offices at 153 Milk Street, Boston, Massachusetts 02109 and
5 Little Road #08-01, Singapore 536983.

Created by Co & Bear Productions (UK) Ltd.
Copyright © 1998 Co & Bear Productions (UK) Ltd.
Photographs copyright © 1998 Sian Irvine.

Library of Congress Cataloging-in-Publication Data
Mushrooms : mushroom recipes by leading chefs from around the globe /
    photographed by Sian Irvine. — 1st ed.
               p.   cm.
    Includes index.
    ISBN 962-593-494-4 (hardcover)
    1. Cookery (Mushrooms) 2. Mushrooms, Edible. I. Irvine, Sian.
TX804.M89   1999   98-47556
641.6'58–dc21   CIP

Distributed by

USA	CANADA
Tuttle Publishing	Raincoast Books
Distribution Center	8680 Cambie Street
Airport Industrial Park	Vancouver, British Columbia
364 Innovation Drive	V6P 6M9
North Clarendon, VT 05759-9436	Tel: (604) 323-7100
Tel: (802) 773-8930	Fax: (604) 323-2600
Tel: (800) 526-2778	

First edition
05 04 03 02 01 00 99   10 9 8 7 6 5 4 3 2
Printed and bound in Italy.

MUSHROOM RECIPES
BY LEADING CHEFS
FROM AROUND THE GLOBE

MUSHROOMS

PHOTOGRAPHED BY
SIAN IRVINE

PERIPLUS

CONTENTS

Mushrooms: From East to West and Beyond

Above: The common brown, one of the most popular of the cultivated fungi.
Opposite: Thousands of varieties of mushroom grow throughout the world's forests, but most people are only familiar with a handful of them.

The cool air of an early morning walk in the woods, an earthy scent rising from the damp ground, the scrunch of golden leaves underfoot: all are autumnal pleasures, but none so thrilling—or ultimately flavorsome—as the hunt for wild mushrooms.

Once foraging was the only way of finding fungi. Now a trip to the supermarket or produce store is as far as the budding mycologist need search for oyster mushrooms, shiitakes, and even the renowned porcini, or *cèpes.* A contemporary fascination with the complex flavors, not to mention the often elusive nature, of these edible fungi has also placed them on the menus of top restaurants.

As this collection of recipes demonstrates, there are few natural foods as versatile, or as globally popular, as the mushroom. Each year, three-quarters of a billion tons of white mushrooms are cultivated in the United States alone. Originally from the Far East, shiitake and enoki are now just as likely to be found in New York and Sydney as Tokyo.

Despite the success of cultivation for a few species, many others—such as the chanterelle and the prized truffle—have so far resisted the challenge, the very best specimens still needing to be hunted out in the forests of Italy and France. If you decide to go foraging yourself, among the 10,000 different types of fungi growing wild in North America alone, only around 250 species are considered worthy as gastronomic delicacies, or even edible.

Finally, a few culinary tips. Bought fresh, mushrooms should generally be used within a couple of days, even if stored in a refrigerator. Most fungi are 90 percent moisture so don't dilute their taste by cleansing in water; instead, use a soft wire brush to scrub them gently free of any dirt. Dried mushrooms, which have a more concentrated flavor, need to be soaked thoroughly before cooking and should be used sparingly. *Simon Richmond*

Chanterelle

Also known as the *girolle* in France, the most common chanterelle (*Cantharellus cibarius*) is a golden honey-colored fungus, although there are also exotic white, black, and even blue varieties. The mushroom blooms, almost flowerlike, in mossy ground from summer through to late autumn, when its yellow color makes it hard to spot among fallen leaves. Its chewy texture and mild flavor are most commonly compared to apricots, although there are also nutty and peppery notes if the mushroom is eaten raw. Cooked, the chanterelle is a splendid accompaniment for eggs, and works well in soups or stewed with meats.

Cultivated White Mushroom

It was the French who first cultivated the *Agaricus brunnescens* in caves near Paris – hence the name of one type, *champignon de Paris* –in the seventeenth century. Now the most commonly found fungi on supermarket shelves come in a variety of sizes, the

smallest being button mushrooms, which have a delicate, yet earthy flavor. They are best used in sauces, sliced raw in salads or marinated whole. Larger varieties have a stronger flavor and a meatier texture, as does the cultivated common brown mushroom, ideal for stuffing, grilling, or frying.

Enoki

Enoki, cultivated in Japan and the United States, are white, strawlike mushrooms with thin, long stems topped with

In mild weather, the morel can sprout from late March through to May on the sandy, chalky soil of woodlands and fields. The pale brown flesh is crisp and moist, with a fine nutty, even bacony, taste. It is the honeycomb texture which absorbs sauces well, and makes the morel so prized by chefs. This is one mushroom that must never be eaten raw, yet stands up well to being dried.

a small cap and are often used as a garnish in soups. The firm flesh, with its crunchy texture, makes this a fine mushroom to serve raw in salads.

Morel

In the same family of fungus as the truffle, morels (*Morchella elata* and *M. esculenta*) are instantly recognizable by their spongy conical caps, although individual mushrooms vary widely in size.

Mousseron

Commonly known as "fairy ring," since they tend to grow in large numbers in a hoop formation. The pale brown mousseron (*Marasmius oreades*) has a slender stem supporting a cap that looks like a mini flying saucer. In season from summer through to autumn, this mushroom's flesh is white with an aroma of dried grass. Tastes best fried with free-range eggs or slowly stewed in a casserole with pork or lamb.

Oyster Mushroom

Now widely available because of successful cultivation, the oyster mushroom (*Pleurotus ostreatus*) is so called because of its creamy gray color and the softly rounded flat shape of the cap. In the wild, this fungus grows in clusters on decaying beech and poplar trees, from early summer through late autumn. The tender white flesh has a delicate, barely perceptible taste that is best used in soups and sauces as a back-up flavor.

Porcini (Cèpe)

The undisputed king of wild mushrooms, the plump, flavorsome porcini (*Boletus edulis*) is also widely known as the *cèpe,* from the French. The Italian name translates as "little pigs," although single specimens have been found that tip the scales at close to a pound (500 g).

Growing in grassy woodland areas from early summer to midautumn, the rounded shape of the the porcino's cap and its just-baked brown color have earned it the name of "penny bun" in Britain.

The firm white flesh has an earthy aroma and a meaty texture. While young, they are best sliced raw for salads or grilled; and when more mature, the slightly tougher porcini cook up well in stews and sauces. This is also an ideal type of mushroom to dry, and a smidgen of dried porcini lifts the flavor of dishes using blander cultivated fungi.

Portobello

The portobello, or fully mature cremino, is a triumph of marketing. The "common brown" is in fact just a relative of the cultivated white mushroom. It does, however, have a more intense taste and firmer texture than the common white, and its wide, flat cap, which opens

with maturity to reveal dark brown gills on the underside, marks the portobello as a particularly good specimen for grilling or sautéing whole.

Shiitake

Cultivated by the Japanese centuries ago, the shiitake (*Lentinula edodes*) is one of the best-known Asian fungi. Its name translates as "oak mushroom," after the tree on which it can be

found growing wild through-out the year. With a broad, flat, beige cap and firm white flesh, the shiitake is a highly versatile mushroom, ideal for a wide range of non-Asian recipes. Dried varieties, which include ones from China that look like ebony buttons, have a smokier flavor than the already earthy taste of fresh shiitake mushrooms.

Trompette de la Mort

Also known as the "horn of plenty," black trumpet or black chanterelle, the trompette de la mort (*Craterellus cornucopiodes*) is a delicate, dusky-gray mushroom, often found close to beech trees. Far from being deadly, the trompette, in season from late summer to late autumn, is edible and can be used as a poor man's substitute for truffles. The gray, thin flesh darkens when cooked, imparting a striking color to dishes, if only subtle mushroom flavoring. Best sautéed or simmered in soups and stews, the trompette also goes well with soft, white fish.

Wood Blewitt

The wood blewitt is a cousin of the expensive Asian matsutake, considered a great delicacy in Japan. The wood blewitt grows in Europe and North America from late summer through to autumn, and its flavor is milder than the intense meaty taste of the matsutake. Not a mushroom to be eaten raw, the wood blewitt is best enjoyed grilled, baked, or stewed, and goes particularly well with rice, eggs, and soy sauce.

east

- Oyster Mushroom Sukha Masala

- Asparagus, Enoki & Chili Salad

- Vegetarian Maki-Zushi with Shiitake & Enoki Mushrooms, Pickles & Avocado

- Zasai Gohan

- Chinese Mushrooms Stir-fried with Chicken Fillet in Sichuan Hot Sauce

- Enoki Mushrooms with Ginger, Garlic & Chili

- Yasai Chili Men

- Mushrooms Manchurian

- Grilled Lemongrass & Ginger Chicken with Cha-Soba

- Oyster Mushrooms in Black Bean Sauce

- Mushroom & Ginger Stir-fry

- Poached Tataki of Tuna with Caramelized Green Onions,
    Mushroom Salad & Ponzu

- Mushrooms in Hot Garlic Sauce

- Wok-Fried Hokkien Noodles with Black Beans, Asian Greens & Shiitake Mushrooms

- Asian Greens with Shiitake Mushrooms & Black Bean Sauce

- Malaysian Mushroom Curry

- Oyster Mushroom & Shiitake Roll

- Crispy Button Mushrooms with Peppercorn, Salt & Chili

- Moyashi Soba

- Tom Kha Hed

- Seared Tuna Sashimi with Shiitake Salad

Oyster Mushroom Sukha Masala

METHOD

1 *Heat the oil over a high heat in a wok or a large saucepan until a haze forms on top.*

2 *Add the mustard seeds and allow to crackle for 30 seconds or until they stop.*

3 *Add the curry leaves along with the cumin seeds, garlic, and green chili, sauté for a minute or so and sprinkle in the asafoetida.*

4 *As soon as the garlic changes color to a pale gold, turn the heat down low and add the chili powder and turmeric. Stir for half a minute, then add the tomatoes.*

5 *Increase the heat and sauté until the tomato skins begin to peel, but the flesh is still firm.*

6 *Increase the heat again and add the mushrooms. Add a few splashes of fresh lime juice, the salt, and cilantro, and toss gently.*

7 *Cook for approximately 2–3 minutes, stirring regularly to prevent sticking. Do not overstir, but ensure that all the mushrooms are tossed well and coated. Check seasoning before serving.*

To serve: *Serve with steamed white rice or fried rice.*

Ingredients

serves 2 with rice

2 tbsp vegetable oil

³/₄ tsp mustard seeds

10–12 curry leaves

1 tsp cumin seeds

4–5 garlic cloves, finely chopped

3 green chilies, seeded & sliced

2 pinches asafoetida

¹/₂ tsp chili powder

¹/₄ tsp ground turmeric

2 medium tomatoes, cut into quarters

6–7 oz (185–220 g) oyster mushrooms

juice of 1 lime

salt to taste

1 tbsp chopped fresh cilantro (coriander)

Note: You can prepare everything well in advance and start cooking about 10 minutes before you are ready to serve.

Asparagus, Enoki & Chili Salad

Ingredients

serves 4 as a starter

12 asparagus spears, trimmed

10 oz (315 g) mixed salad greens

4 avocados, quartered & fanned

4 oz (125 g) enoki mushrooms

4 fresh chives, cut into segments

for the chili hollandaise

2 egg yolks

1 tsp chili purée

4 tbsp (2 oz/60 g) butter, softened

pinch of salt

$^1/_2$ tsp lime juice

for the vinaigrette

1 tbsp soy sauce

1 tbsp truffle juice

1 tbsp lemon juice

salt & pepper

5 tbsp (2$^1/_2$ fl oz/75 ml) olive oil

METHOD

1 *Make the hollandaise dressing in advance. Whisk the egg yolks and chili in a bowl over hot water until thick. Whisk in the butter and season with salt and lime juice.*

2 *Next, mix all the vinaigrette ingredients, except the oil, together in a bowl. Slowly drizzle in the oil while whisking.*

3 *Set aside the hollandaise and vinaigrette while you parboil the asparagus. Bring a medium-sized saucepan of water to a boil and add the asparagus. Bring quickly back to a boil and cook for 2–3 minutes, then drain.*

4 *Arrange some of the salad greens on each serving plate. Season with the vinaigrette. Arrange the avocados, enoki, and asparagus on top.*

To serve: *Dress the asparagus with a spoonful of the hollandaise sauce and garnish with chives.*

Vegetarian Maki-Zushi with Shiitake & Enoki Mushrooms, Pickles & Avocado

METHOD

1 *Prepare the sushi rice in advance. Wash the rice in a colander with cold running water until the water runs clear. Place the rice in a saucepan with the water, the konbu and sake. Cover with a tight-fitting lid and bring to a boil.*

2 *Remove the konbu and replace the lid. Turn the heat to low and cook for 15 minutes, then remove from the heat and leave the rice to steam for a further 10–15 minutes.*

3 *Using a wooden spoon, transfer the rice to a bowl. Mix the sugar and salt into the vinegar, then quickly and gently stir into the rice. Cover the rice with a damp tea towel and leave to cool for about 15 minutes.*

4 *Meanwhile, heat the vegetable oil in a wok over medium heat and stir-fry the mushrooms for 3 minutes, tossing regularly. Set aside.*

5 *Lay half a sheet of nori on a sushi rolling mat, with the smooth side of the nori facing down. Wet fingers in cold water, then evenly spread the rice over the nori, leaving a finger's width border at the base.*

6 *Gently turn over the nori so that the moist rice is now facing down on the mat. Using the back of a teaspoon, smear a thin trail of wasabi across the middle of the nori about halfway up the sheet. Lay a quarter of the filling ingredients—mushrooms, spinach, daikon, carrot, and avocado—on top of the wasabi. Then fold the mat away from you to bring the nori and rice layer up over the filling. Roll the mat up tightly to form a tube, taking care to ensure that the filling is kept inside.*

7 *Unroll the sushi mat and you will be left with a sausage-shaped sushi roll. Repeat with the remaining nori.*

8 *Once all 4 sheets have been used, roll each sushi in chopped chives and cress. Dip a sharp knife into water and slice each sushi roll into 8 equal portions.*

To serve: *Arrange several pieces of sushi on each plate, and serve with pickled ginger in one small dish, soy sauce in another, and a dab of wasabi on another. The traditional way of eating sushi is to dissolve a tiny piece of wasabi in the saucer of soy sauce and dip the sushi into it immediately before eating.*

Ingredients

serves 6–8

for the rice

1³/₄ cups (10 oz/315 g) short-grain sushi rice

1¹/₂ cups (12 fl oz/375 ml) water

3-inch (7.5-cm) piece konbu seaweed

1 tbsp sake or dry white wine

1 tbsp superfine (caster) sugar

1 tsp salt

1¹/₂ tbsp rice vinegar

for the sushi

1 tbsp vegetable oil

4 oz (125 g) mixed shiitake & enoki mushrooms, chopped

4 sheets nori seaweed, cut in half

1 tsp prepared wasabi

2 oz (60 g) spinach, cooked

4 oz (125 g) piece pickled Japanese daikon, thinly sliced

1 medium carrot, peeled & cut into very fine strips

1 avocado, finely diced

4 fresh chives, chopped

small handful cress, chopped

accompaniments

1 small bag pickled ginger

1 small bottle soy sauce

1 tsp prepared wasabi

Ingredients

serves 4

4 chicken breast halves, skinned & boned

2 tbsp vegetable oil

2 tbsp garlic paste

4 oz (125 g) Japanese pickled cabbage

3 oz (90 g) Sichuan preserved vegetables

3 oz (90 g) shiitake mushrooms, sliced

2 cups (16 fl oz/500 ml) water

pinch of salt

3 tbsp sugar

3 tbsp oyster sauce

3 tbsp light soy sauce

arrowroot or potato starch, to thicken if needed

1 bunch green (spring) onions, thinly sliced at an angle

4 cups ($1^3/_4$ lb/875 g) hot cooked white rice, preferably organic

$^2/_3$ cup (4 oz/125 g) hot cooked wild rice

4 tsp chili paste for garnish

Zasai Gohan

METHOD

1 *Poach the chicken breasts in water to cover for 8–10 minutes. Allow to cool and then slice into thin strips.*

2 *To make the sauce, heat the oil in a wok, add the garlic paste, and cook very gently without allowing the paste to color. Add the chicken, pickled and preserved vegetables, and shiitake mushrooms and mix well.*

3 *Add the water to the wok and bring to a boil as quickly as possible. Season with the salt, sugar, oyster sauce, and soy sauce. Taste and adjust seasoning if necessary. If the sauce is too thin, add a little arrowroot or potato starch to thicken.*

4 *When the sauce reaches the desired consistency, sprinkle in the green onions and remove from the heat.*

To serve: *Mix together the cooked rices and divide among 4 bowls. Immediately pour the chicken sauce over the rice. Top each dish with a teaspoon of chili paste to garnish.*

Chinese Mushrooms Stir-fried with Chicken Fillet in Sichuan Hot Sauce

Ingredients

serves 1 with rice

2 oz (60 g) dried black Chinese mushrooms (shiitake)

1 chicken breast half, boned and thinly sliced

$^{1}/_{2}$ tbsp cornstarch (cornflour)

$^{1}/_{2}$ tsp salt

2 cups (16 fl oz/500 ml) chicken stock

3 tbsp vegetable oil

$^{1}/_{2}$ tsp crushed garlic

3 tbsp tomato ketchup

1 tbsp chili sauce

1 tsp superfine (caster) sugar

1 tsp light soy sauce

2 shallots, finely chopped

METHOD

1 *Soak the mushrooms in hot water for 30 minutes, then wash them under cold water and put to one side.*

2 *Mix the sliced chicken breast, cornstarch, and salt and leave for 15 minutes.*

3 *Boil the mushrooms in the chicken stock for about 10 minutes, or until tender. Drain and put to one side.*

4 *Heat 2 tablespoons of the vegetable oil in a wok and fry the chicken until it is cooked. Remove the chicken from the pan, drain and put to one side.*

5 *About 10 minutes before you wish to serve, cook the rest of the dish. Heat the remaining 1 tablespoon oil in the wok over high heat. Reduce the heat to medium, add the garlic and cook until it turns pale gold.*

6 *Remove the wok from the heat and add the tomato ketchup, chili sauce, sugar and soy sauce. Return to medium heat and stir until the sugar melts.*

7 *Add the chicken and mushrooms to the sauce in the wok and stir to mix and heat through, about 1 minute.*

To serve: *Ladle into a shallow bowl and finish with a sprinkling of chopped shallots. Serve with a side dish of rice.*

Enoki Mushrooms with Ginger, Garlic & Chili

Ingredients

serves 2

1 cup (8 fl oz/250 ml)
vegetable oil

2 yellow onions, thinly sliced

6–7 oz (185–220 g) okra

$^1/_2$ tsp chaat masala

1 tsp cumin seeds

6–8 curry leaves, finely
shredded

4 or 5 garlic cloves, chopped

1$^1/_4$-inch (3-cm) piece ginger,
peeled & finely shredded

3 green (spring) onions,
shredded

2 green chilies, seeded &
finely shredded

4 oz (125 g) enoki mushrooms

$^1/_2$ tsp lemon juice

pinch of salt

1 medium to large tomato,
seeded & julienned

2 tbsp finely chopped fresh
cilantro (fresh coriander)

METHOD

1 *Before you start to cook, place a sieve over a stainless-steel or heat-resistant glass bowl and keep ready for use.*

2 *Heat the oil in a wok. When it is just hot, add the yellow onions, stirring almost continuously until they turn a light golden brown. Pour immediately into the sieve (Do not try to remove them from the pan a spoonful at a time or the color will not be even.)*

3 *Spread the onions out in the sieve with a fork to release any trapped heat. If this is not done, the onions will continue to brown with the latent heat. Reserve the oil that filters through to the bowl below.*

4 *Meanwhile, trim the okra and slice them very thinly lengthwise.*

5 *Transfer the fried onions to a plate or bowl lined with paper towels.*

6 *Return the strained oil to the wok and reheat it until just hot. Fry the okra until pale gold in color, pouring into the*

Recipe continued on following page

Recipe continued from previous page...

sieve when ready. Again, reserve the oil that collects in the bowl.

7 *When both onions and okra have cooled, they will turn crisp. Mix both in a bowl and sprinkle with chaat masala.*

8 *Clean the wok of any residue and return to the heat. Add 2 tablespoons of the strained oil and heat to the smoking point. Add the cumin seeds and curry leaves, and almost immediately add the chopped garlic, ginger, green onions, and green chilies. Toss constantly for a minute or two without reducing the heat.*

9 *Add the mushrooms and toss for a further minute.*

10 *Add the lemon juice, salt, and tomato. Mix well and check the seasoning.*

11 *Sprinkle in most of the chopped cilantro and remove the wok from the heat. Add the remaining cilantro to the okra and onions.*

To serve: *Arrange a bed of the crispy okra and onion pieces on each plate and spoon a generous helping of the mushrooms on top.*

Yasai Chili Mein

METHOD

1 *Start by making the sauce. In a blender, combine the peppers, lemongrass, ginger, onion, chilies, and garlic and blend until smooth. Place in a fine sieve over a bowl to let the excess water drain off.*

2 *Heat 1 tablespoon of the oil in a pan and add the blended mixture. Then add the sugar, chili and garlic sauce, soy sauce, and ketchup. Season with salt. Fry gently for 30–40 minutes, or until the mixture thickens and the oil turns red.*

3 *Next, heat a tablespoon of oil in a wok and fry the carrots over low heat for 2–3 minutes. Turn up the heat, add the swow peas, mushrooms and tofu, and cook for a further 2 minutes. Add the blended sauce, zucchini and tomatoes, and simmer gently while you cook the noodles.*

4 *If using fresh noodles, gently ease them apart before placing in a large pan of boiling salted water. Bring back to the boil and cook for 45 seconds, stirring constantly. For dried noodles, cook according to packet instructions.*

To serve: *Drain the noodles and divide among 4 bowls. Pour the sauce over, garnishing with the chopped green onions.*

Recipe photograph on following page...

Ingredients

serves 4

1 tbsp vegetable oil

3 medium carrots, peeled & thinly sliced

4 oz (125 g) snow peas (mangetouts)

4 oz (125 g) button mushrooms, thinly sliced

12 cubes fried tofu, ($^{1}/_{2}$-inch/12-mm cubes)

4 oz (125 g) zucchini (courgettes), halved & thinly sliced at an angle

2 medium tomatoes, cut into 12 pieces

10 oz (315 g) Chinese noodles

1 bunch green (spring) onions, sliced at an angle

for the sauce

6 large red bell peppers (capsicums), seeded & chopped

2 lemongrass stalks trimmed & crushed

2-oz (60-g) piece ginger, crushed

1 large onion, chopped

4 large red chilies, seeded & chopped

2 cloves garlic, crushed

1 tbsp vegetable oil

$^{1}/_{4}$ cup (2 oz/60 g) sugar

$^{3}/_{4}$ cup (6 fl oz/180 ml) chili & garlic sauce

$^{1}/_{4}$ cup (2 fl oz/60 ml) light soy sauce

2 tbsp tomato ketchup

salt to taste

Yasai Chili Mein

(recipe on preceding page)

Mushrooms Manchurian

Ingredients

serves 2 with rice

2–3 tbsp vegetable oil

2 star anise

2 red chilies, chopped into small pieces

14 oz (440 g) button mushrooms, trimmed a little at the base

1¹/₂ tbsp finely chopped garlic

1 tbsp very finely chopped ginger

2 or 3 green chilies, finely chopped

4 thin green (spring) onions, chopped

1 medium carrot, peeled & finely chopped

1 green bell pepper (capsicum), diced

³/₄ cup (6 fl oz/180 ml) vegetable stock or water

few drops dark soy sauce

salt & pepper

1–2 tbsp cornstarch (cornflour)

2–3 tbsp cold water

1 tbsp finely chopped fresh cilantro (coriander)

Note: Remember that once the cornstarch is added, the dish will not reheat well, as the starch from the flour begins to break up. It is advisable to add the cornstarch just before serving.

METHOD

1 *Before you start to cook, place a sieve over a stainless-steel or heat-resistant glass bowl and keep ready for use.*

2 *Heat the oil in a wok or large saucepan until a haze forms on top.*

3 *Add the star anise and fry for a few seconds before adding the red chili pieces. As soon as the chilies are dark, but not burned, add the mushrooms and fry for 1–2 minutes over high heat.*

4 *Drain the contents of the wok into the sieve and wipe the rim of the wok to mop up any oil drips.*

5 *Return the strained oil to the wok over high heat. Add the garlic, ginger, green chilies, green onions, carrot, and bell pepper, and sauté for a minute or two. Add the stock or water, soy sauce, salt and pepper, and bring to a boil.*

6 *Meanwhile, mix the cornstarch in a cup with the water until you get a smooth paste.*

7 *When the contents of the wok begins to boil, add the fried mushroom mixture and bring to a boil again. Add the cornstarch paste a little at a time, stirring continuously, until the sauce thickens to the desired consistency.*

8 *Check the seasoning, add the cilantro and mix well.*

To serve: *Serve with steamed white rice or fried rice.*

Grilled Lemongrass & Ginger Chicken with Cha-Soba

Ingredients

serves 4

4–6 chicken thighs, boned & skinned

4 oz (125 g) dried cha-soba noodles

12 shiitake mushrooms, stems removed

scant 1 cup (7 fl oz/220 ml) store-bought ponzu dressing

2 green (spring) onions, thinly sliced

handful purple shiso leaves (optional)

for the marinade

1 lemongrass stalk, trimmed & thinly sliced

1-inch (2.5-cm) piece ginger, peeled & thinly sliced

$^1/_4$ cup (2 fl oz/60 ml) sunflower oil

1 tsp superfine (caster) sugar

1 tbsp soy sauce

Note: Cha-soba noodles, ponzu, and shiso leaves are generally available at Japanese markets and at health-food stores.

METHOD

1 *Put all the marinade ingredients in a blender, reserving $^1/_2$ tablespoon of the oil, and blend until smooth.*

2 *Coat the chicken thighs well with the marinade, cover with plastic wrap and refrigerate for at least 4 hours.*

3 *Bring a large pan of salted water to a boil, gradually pour in the cha-soba noodles and stir well. Bring back to the boil and add a cup of cold water. Bring back to the boil a second time and again add a cup of cold water. Repeat this process once more, then drain the cha-soba and rinse well under cold running water to remove any excess starch.*

4 *Cook chicken thighs under a hot broiler (griller) until golden and cooked through; this should take 12–15 minutes.*

5 *While the chicken broils (grills), slice the shiitake mushrooms and sauté in a nonstick pan with the reserved $^1/_2$ tablespoon sunflower oil. Allow to cool a little before serving.*

To serve: *Toss the cha-soba in a little of the ponzu dressing, then place a portion of the noodles on each plate. Top with the cooked mushrooms, then slice each chicken thigh into 4 pieces and carefully arrange on top of the mushrooms. Pour a tablespoon of ponzu dressing over the chicken and sprinkle with green onions and with a few purple shiso leaves, if desired.*

Oyster Mushrooms in Black Bean Sauce

METHOD

1 *Halve the mushrooms.*

2 *Place the mushrooms in a saucepan of boiling water for 30 seconds, then drain and put to one side.*

3 *Gently wash the black beans in a small bowl of water to clean them. Drain and then mash with a teaspoon.*

4 *Mix the onion, green onion, black beans, garlic, and ginger in a bowl.*

5 *In a separate bowl, mix the light soy sauce, dark soy sauce, and oyster sauce.*

6 *Heat the vegetable oil in a wok. Lightly fry the onion mixture over medium to high heat for a minute. Add the mushrooms and cook over high heat until sizzling.*

7 *Pour in the soy sauce mixture and bring to a boil.*

8 *Stir in the cornstarch paste and quickly fry until the sauce thickens to a gravy.*

To serve: *Serve with steamed white rice.*

Ingredients

serves 2 with rice

10 oz (315 g) oyster mushrooms

2 tsp salted black beans

2 tsp finely chopped onion

2 tsp finely chopped green (spring) onion

1 garlic clove, crushed

$^1/_2$ tsp crushed ginger

$^1/_2$ tbsp light soy sauce

$^1/_2$ tbsp dark soy sauce

1 tbsp oyster sauce

2 tbsp vegetable oil

1 tbsp cornstarch (cornflour) mixed into 4 tbsp (2 fl oz/60 ml) water

Mushroom & Ginger Stir-fry

METHOD

1 *Heat the shallot oil in a wok over a medium heat. When it is just hot, add the onion and ginger, stirring quickly so they do not burn.*

2 *Quickly add the mushrooms and mixed peppers, briskly stirring the ingredients around in the wok.*

3 *Add the oyster sauce, soy sauce, and sugar and stir.*

4 *Cook over medium heat, stirring constantly for about a minute, or until the mushrooms are cooked.*

5 *Add the green onion and chili and stir in well. Then remove wok from heat and serve immediately.*

To serve: *Serve with steamed white rice.*

Ingredients

serves 1 with rice

1 tbsp shallot oil

$^1/_4$ red onion, finely chopped

$^3/_4$-inch (2-cm) piece ginger, peeled & thinly sliced

1 clove garlic, finely chopped

5 oz (155 g) mixed mushrooms (oyster, wood blewitt, enoki), thickly sliced

$^1/_4$ red bell pepper (capsicum), diced

$^1/_4$ yellow bell pepper (capsicum), diced

$^3/_4$ tbsp oyster sauce

$^3/_4$ tbsp soy sauce

$^1/_4$ tsp sugar

1 green (spring) onion, thinly sliced diagonally

4 or 5 slices red chili

Poached Tataki of Tuna with Caramelized Green Onions, Mushroom Salad & Ponzu

Ingredients

serves 4

2 tbsp mirin (sweet rice wine)

1 tbsp rice vinegar

2 tbsp sunflower oil

pinch salt

4 oz (125 g) button mushrooms, thinly sliced

10 oz (315 g) tuna fillet

6 green (spring) onions, trimmed & cut in half

scant 1 cup (7 fl oz/220 ml) store-bought ponzu dressing

1-inch (2.5-cm) piece ginger, peeled & cut into very fine strips

small handful cress

pinch of coarse sea salt

METHOD

1 *Mix 1 tablespoon of the mirin with the rice vinegar and sunflower oil and add a pinch of salt to make the dressing. Place the sliced button mushrooms into a small bowl and toss with the dressing. Refrigerate for at least 15 minutes before serving.*

2 *Bring a pan of well-salted water to a boil and immerse the tuna fillet for 15 seconds. Then remove and place immediately into iced water. When cold, drain and dry with kitchen towels. Cut into slices $^1/_4$-inch (6-mm) thick with a sharp knife. Refrigerate until needed.*

3 *Toss the green onions in the remaining 1 tablespoon mirin, then place on a baking sheet (tray) under a hot broiler (griller) and cook for a few minutes until caramelized. Remove the green onions and allow to cool a little.*

To serve: *Place a little mushroom salad in the center of 4 serving plates, top with 3 or 4 slices of tuna, then drizzle over a good tablespoon or two of ponzu dressing. Place 3 pieces of caramelized green onion on top of the tuna, followed by a few strips of fresh ginger and some cress. Season with a pinch of sea salt.*

Mushrooms in Hot Garlic Sauce

METHOD

1 *Start cooking about 10–12 minutes before you are ready to serve. Heat the oil in a wok over a medium heat. Add the garlic and sauté for a minute until golden.*

2 *Add the ginger and green chilies and continue to sauté for a further 2 minutes. Add the tomatoes, the sugar, and the vinegar to taste and cook until the sauce thickens.*

3 *Add the green onions, season, and check for taste. The sauce should be slightly sweet but quite hot, sour, and garlicky.*

4 *When the sauce is quite thick, increase the heat, add the mushrooms, and cook for no more than 2-3 minutes on high, stirring almost continuously.*

5 *Once the mushrooms are fully coated and heated through, remove from the heat and serve immediately.*

To serve: *Sprinkle with the cilantro and serve with fried rice.*

Ingredients

serves 2 with rice

2 tbsp vegetable oil

8–10 cloves garlic, chopped

2-inch (5-cm) piece ginger, peeled & finely chopped

3 or 4 green chilies, chopped

4 or 5 medium tomatoes, peeled & chopped

2 tsp sugar

1–2 tbsp white vinegar, to taste

3 green (spring) onions, finely chopped

salt to taste

8 oz (250 g) mixed mushrooms, sliced

$^1/_2$ tbsp finely chopped fresh cilantro (coriander)

Wok-Fried Hokkien Noodles with Black Beans, Asian Greens & Shiitake Mushrooms

Ingredients

serves 1

1 tbsp shallot oil

pinch finely chopped ginger

$^1/_4$ red onion, finely sliced

1 tbsp light soy sauce

$^1/_2$ tsp sugar

1 tsp black bean & chili paste

10 oz (315 g) Hokkien, Shanghai, or other fresh, pre-cooked, thick wheat noodles

2–3 tbsp water, as needed

3 large shiitake mushrooms, thinly sliced

1 handful Asian greens (bok choy), chopped into 2-inch (5-cm) lengths

METHOD

1 *Pour the shallot oil into a hot wok and add the ginger and red onion.*

2 *Add the soy sauce, sugar, black bean and chili paste, and noodles, stirring all the time until the noodles are completely coated. Add a little water to help the cooking of the noodles. This will also prevent them sticking to the wok.*

3 *To complete the dish, stir in the mushrooms and greens. Toss several times. Remove from the heat as soon as the mushrooms and greens are coated and just cooked.*

To serve: *Serve immediately in a large bowl.*

Asian Greens with Shiitake Mushrooms & Black Bean Sauce

METHOD

1 *Heat a wok over high heat and add half of the shallot oil.*

2 *Add the ginger and fry for 20 seconds.*

3 *Add the black bean sauce, water or chicken broth, and sugar. Stir in the mushrooms and cook for 2 minutes, or until the liquid has reduced.*

4 *Add the greens and soy sauce and cook for 1 minute, or until the leaves have turned dark green.*

3 *Remove the wok from the heat and serve immediately.*

To serve: *Lay the greens on a serving plate. Remove the mushrooms from the sauce and arrange on top. Then spoon the sauce over the top.*

Ingredients

serves 2 as a side dish

1 tbsp shallot oil

$^1/_2$-inch (12-mm) piece ginger, peeled & thinly sliced

1 tbsp black bean sauce

1 tbsp water or chicken broth

pinch of sugar

4 large shiitake mushrooms

1 large handful Asian greens (bok choy)

$^1/_2$ tbsp light soy sauce

Malaysian Mushroom Curry

METHOD

1 *Heat a wok over medium heat and pour in the shallot oil. Add the garlic, onion, and lemongrass and fry for a few seconds.*

2 *Add the curry powder and fry for 20 seconds, taking care not to burn it.*

3 *Add the oyster sauce and coconut milk, then cook for 1 minute.*

4 *Add the mushrooms and the remaining vegetables. Stir in the sugar, water and chili and cook for 2–3 minutes, or until the vegetables are cooked and the liquid thickens.*

To serve: *Ladle into a deep bowl and serve with steamed rice.*

Ingredients

serves 1 with rice

1 tbsp shallot oil

1 clove garlic

$^1/_2$ red onion, diced

$^1/_2$ lemongrass stalk, trimmed & thinly sliced

$^1/_2$ tsp medium-hot curry powder (Malaysian if possible)

2 tsp oyster sauce

4 tbsp (2 fl oz/60 ml) coconut milk

5 oz (150 g) oyster mushrooms

$^1/_4$ red bell pepper (capsicum), seeded & diced

$^1/_4$ yellow bell pepper (capsicum), seeded & diced

$^1/_2$ tomato, quartered

pinch sugar

2 tsp water

2 slices red chili

Oyster Mushroom & Shiitake Roll

Ingredients

serves 4

1¼ cups (9 oz/280 g) short-grain sushi rice

½ cup (4 fl oz/125 ml) store-bought seasoned rice vinegar

1 tbsp sunflower oil

8 oz (250 g) oyster mushrooms

8 oz (250 g) shiitake mushrooms, halved

1 large shallot, finely diced

1 small red chili, chopped

2 cloves garlic, crushed

3 tbsp soy sauce

4 sheets nori seaweed

12 fresh chive

3 tbsp all-purpose (plain) flour

1 egg, beaten

Japanese bread crumbs (panko)

vegetable oil for deep-frying

purple sprouting broccoli, or green broccoli chopped into florets

2 tbsp store-bought ponzu dressing

2 tsp sesame seeds

METHOD

1 *Wash the rice well and soak for 30 minutes, then cook in a rice cooker, or boil gently for 30 minutes. Transfer to a bowl and gently stir in the rice vinegar. Let cool.*

2 *Heat the sunflower oil in a wok and fry the mushrooms with the shallot, chili, and garlic for 2 minutes. Add 1 tablespoon of the soy sauce and remove from the heat. Transfer to a sieve over a bowl; let cool.*

3 *To roll the sushi, lay 1 sheet of nori on the sushi rolling mat. Wet hands and press the rice in a layer ¼ inch (6 mm) thick over two-thirds of the nori, leaving a border around the edge of the sheet. Place the 12 whole chives evenly spaced across the rice, then a quarter of the mushrooms along the edge nearest to you. Fold the mat over the filling and roll it up so that the nori is pulled into the tube. Unroll the mat and twist the ends of the nori like a Christmas cracker.*

4 *When you have made 4 rolls, coat each in flour, egg and bread crumbs. Deep fry at 375°F (180°C) for 5 minutes. If you do not have a deep fryer, fry in 1 inch (2.5 cm) of hot vegetable oil in a heavy saucepan. Remove and drain on paper towels. Leave to cool, then cut each roll into 4 pieces.*

5 *Stir-fry the broccoli in a wok with the remaining soy sauce and ponzu.*

To serve: *Place some broccoli on each plate with a little soy from the wok. Stack 4 sushi pieces along side and sprinkle with sesame seeds.*

Crispy Button Mushrooms with Peppercorn, Salt & Chili

Ingredients

serves 2 as a starter

6–7 oz (185–220 g) button mushrooms

1 red chili

1 green (spring) onion

juice of $^1\!/_2$ lemon, or 1 tbsp vinegar

2 tsp salt

$^1\!/_2$ tsp chicken stock base

generous pinch of coarse ground pepper

3 tbsp self-rising flour

4 tbsp (1 oz/30 g) cornstarch (cornflour)

4 tbsp (2 fl oz/60 ml) vegetable oil

4 tbsp (2 fl oz/60 ml) water

vegetable oil for deep-frying

2 large leaves iceberg lettuce

1 shallot, finely chopped

METHOD

1 *Halve the mushrooms. Cut the chili and green onion into rounds or small pieces. (After chopping the chili use the lemon juice or vinegar to clean fingers.)*

2 *Mix the salt, chicken stock base, and pepper in a bowl. In a separate bowl, mix the self-rising flour, cornstarch, 3 tablespoons of vegetable oil, and the water. Then mix the flour paste and mushrooms together in a bowl.*

3 *Deep-fry the mushrooms, placing them in the fryer one at a time so that they cook separately. If not using a deep fryer, cook in 1 inch (2.5 cm) of the oil in a heavy saucepan. Fry each mushroom until crispy and golden brown. Remove from fryer and drain on paper towels.*

4 *Heat 1 tablespoon of oil in a wok. Throw in the chili and green onion and stir-fry for 30 seconds.*

5 *Add the deep-fried mushrooms to the wok, tossing continuously. Sprinkle the chicken stock base mixture into the mushrooms and stir-fry for about a minute, or until the chili and onion are mixed with the mushrooms.*

To serve: *Spoon the mushrooms into 2 small bowls, each lined with a large lettuce leaf. Garnish with the chopped shallot.*

Moyashi Soba

Ingredients

serves 4

2¹/₂ qt (2.5 l) vegetable stock

1 tbsp vegetable oil

1 clove garlic, crushed

5 oz (150 g) button mushrooms, thinly sliced

4 oz (125 g) snow peas (mangetouts), halved diagonally

4 oz (125 g) leek, white part only, cut in half lengthwise and sliced diagonally

1 lb (500 g) bean sprouts

4 oz (125 g) zucchini (courgettes), cut in half length-wise and sliced diagonally

12 cubes fried tofu (¹/₂-inch/12-mm cubes)

cornstarch (cornflour) or potato starch, for thickening

1 tsp light soy sauce

salt to taste

1 tsp sugar, or to taste

1 lb (500 g) fresh or dried soba noodles

2 oz (60 g) enoki mushrooms

1 bunch green (spring) onions, thinly sliced

METHOD

1 *Heat the vegetable stock gently in a pan.*

2 *Meanwhile, heat the oil in a wok and gently cook the garlic without letting it color. Add the water and bring to a boil.*

3 *Add the button mushrooms, snow peas, leek, bean sprouts, zucchini and tofu, and mix. Bring back to a boil and cook for 4–5 minutes, adding the cornstarch to thicken as desired. Season to taste with soy sauce, salt and sugar. Keep warm while you cook the noodles.*

4 *If using fresh noodles, loosen them by easing gently apart and then place in a big pot of salted boiling water. Bring back to a boil and cook for about 45 seconds, stirring all the while. If using dried noodles, cook according to packet instructions. Drain and serve immediately.*

To serve: *Divide the noodles among 4 bowls, and add the vegetable stock. Spoon the wok mixture over the noodles and garnish with the enoki mushrooms and green onions.*

Tom Kha Hed

Ingredients

serves 1

1 cup (8 fl oz/250 ml) chicken stock, preferably homemade

$1/2$ shallot, bruised with knife

small piece galanga sliced diagonally into strips $1^1/_2$ inches (4 cm) wide

$1/4$ lemongrass stalk, trimmed and sliced diagonally into 2-inch (5-cm) pieces

2 Kaffir lime leaves, cut into strips

2 tsp Thai squid fish sauce

$1/2$ tsp sugar

few button mushrooms, quartered

4 tbsp (2 fl oz/60 ml) coconut milk

4 slices red chili

juice of $1/2$ lime

1 green (spring) onion, thinly sliced diagonally

1 fresh cilantro (coriander) sprig, chopped

few drops chili oil (optional)

METHOD

1 *Heat the wok over medium heat and pour in the chicken stock.*

2 *Add the shallot, galanga, lemongrass, and lime leaves. Cook for 30 seconds.*

3 *Add the fish sauce, sugar, mushrooms, and coconut milk, and boil for 2 minutes.*

4 *Toss in the chili slices and the lime juice, and remove from the heat.*

To serve: *Ladle into a large soup bowl and garnish with the green onion and cilantro. Finish with a few drops of chili oil, if desired and serve with steamed rice.*

Seared Tuna Sashimi with Shiitake Salad

METHOD

1 *Roll the tuna in five-spice powder. Heat a heavy metal frying pan until very hot and sear the tuna for 20 seconds on each side. Remove and chill in the refrigerator.*

2 *Next heat the sunflower oil to 325°F (165°C) and deep-fry the lotus root until golden. Drain on paper towels.*

3 *Assemble all the salad ingredients in a bowl. Mix all the salad dressing ingredients together with a fork and use half of it to dress the salad.*

4 *Thread 4 bamboo skewers with alternate slices of lotus root and pickled ginger. Finish with a lime wedge on the tip of the skewer.*

To serve: *Thinly slice the chilled tuna, and divide among 4 plates. Arrange a small pile of salad on each plate and drizzle over the remaining dressing. Place 1 of the prepared skewers on each plate, along with a small blob of wasabi and 2 shiso leaves to decorate.*

Ingredients

serves 4

6–7 oz (185–220 g) tuna loin, in one piece

1 tsp five-spice powder

sunflower oil for deep-frying

4-inch (10-cm) piece lotus root, thinly sliced on a mandoline

1 small bag pickled ginger

1 lime, cut into quarters

1 tsp prepared wasabi

8 shiso leaves

for the salad

8 shiitake mushrooms, thinly sliced

3 green (spring) onions, thinly sliced

4-oz (125-g) piece daikon, shredded

$1/2$ cucumber, shredded

for the dressing

2 tbsp soy sauce

1 tsp Asian sesame oil

1 tsp sunflower oil

juice of 1 lime

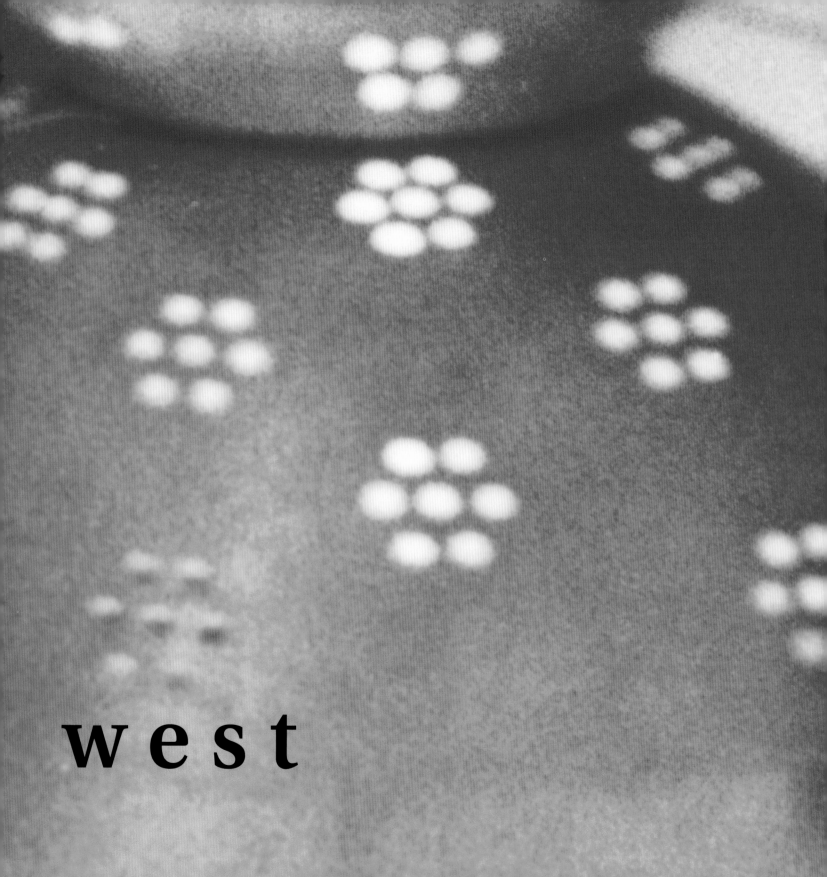

west

- Grilled Mushrooms on Texas Toast with Texas Steak Sauce

- Mushroom Ragout Surprise

- Wild Morel Tamale with Pico de Gallo & Cilantro Oil

- Monkfish, Clams, Samphire & Trompettes de la Mort

- Squab, Wild Mushroom & Barolo Risotto

- Pork Sausage with Purée of Caramelized Cauliflower

- Roast Lamb with Wild Mushroom Hash Browns

- Roast Cod with a Casserole of Shrimp, White Beans & Mushroom Sauce

- Crepinette of Scallops, Spinach & Porcini with Velouté of Fava Beans & Morels

- Carpaccio of Beef, Bruschetta & Wild Mushrooms

- Lasagna of Shrimp, Pig's Trotters & Truffles

- Millefeuille of Salmon, Leek & Seasonal Wild Mushrooms

- Wild Mushrooms on Thyme Rösti with Leek Sprouts & Sour Cream

- Herb Tagliatelle with Baby Clams, Garlic & Porcini Mushrooms

- Crostini with Chanterelles, Poached Egg & Pesto Dressing

- Roasted Porcini Feuillentine

- Roast Rabbit Leg with Olives, Thyme & Portobello Mushrooms

- Saucisson de Foie Gras & Champignons Sauvages

- Risotto of Foie Gras & Truffles

- Ragout of Mushrooms, Warm Poached Eggs & Black Truffles

- Paris Mushroom, Fennel & Parmesan Salad

- Giant Portobello Mushrooms with Artichoke Stew

- Tagliatelle with Morel Mushrooms & Cream

- Terrine of Porcini & Herbs

- Cannellini & Porcini Soup

Ingredients

serves 4

1 lb (500 g) mixed large
wild mushrooms of choice

1/2 cup (4 fl oz/125 ml) olive oil

salt & pepper

4 thick slices ciabatta or other
coarse country bread

1 clove garlic

2–3 tbsp olive oil for bread

2 tbsp butter

2 tbsp sherry

2 tbsp chopped fresh parsley

for the Texas steak sauce

1 tbsp tamarind paste

2 tbsp brown sugar

1/2 cup (5 oz/155 g) tomato
ketchup

6 tbsp (3 fl oz/90 ml) ketjap
manis (Indonesian sweetened
soy sauce)

2 tbsp chili powder

4 tbsp (2 fl oz/60 ml) rice
vinegar

3/4 cup (6 fl oz/180 ml) water

1 tbsp minced ginger

1 clove garlic, finely chopped

pepper to taste

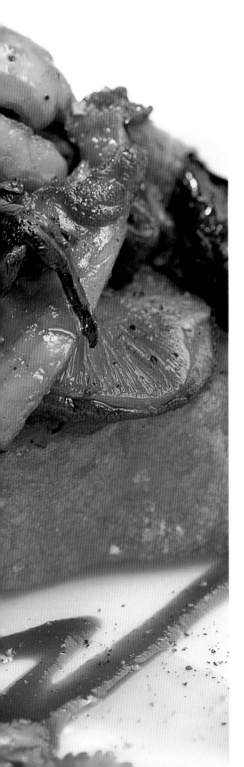

Grilled Mushrooms on Texas Toast with Texas Steak Sauce

METHOD

1 *Make the Texas steak sauce in advance, combining the ingredients in a saucepan and simmering over low heat for around 30 minutes, or until it reaches the consistency of tomato ketchup. Warm the sauce gently prior to serving.*

2 *Wipe the mushrooms with a damp towel and cut off any tough stems. Toss in a bowl with the olive oil and a little salt and black pepper until most of the oil is absorbed.*

3 *Grill the mushrooms over a charcoal fire or under a broiler (griller), turning occasionally until brown and crispy.*

4 *Meanwhile, rub the bread with the garlic clove, brush with the olive oil, and toast until golden brown.*

5 *When the mushrooms are ready, return them to the bowl and toss with the butter, sherry, and parsley until the butter has melted.*

To serve: *Pile a quarter of the mushrooms on top of each piece of toast. Pour a ring of steak sauce around each serving.*

Ingredients

serves 4

6 egg whites

1 tsp chopped tarragon

1 cup (5 oz/155 g) frozen peas

4 oz (125 g) small button mushrooms

4 oz (125 g) chanterelle girolle mushrooms

knob of butter

juice of $^1/_2$ lemon

1 clove garlic, crushed

salt & pepper

$^2/_3$ cup (4 oz/125 g) diced tomato

1 tbsp chopped fresh parsley

1 tbsp chopped fresh chives

1 cup (4 oz/125 g) shelled, blanched fava (broad) beans

3 tbsp crème fraîche

4 fresh chives, chopped, for garnish

for the sabayon

3 egg yolks

1 tbsp vinegar

3 tbsp hot water

3 tbsp butter, melted

Mushroom Ragout Surprise

METHOD

1 *Beat the egg whites until stiff, mixing in the chopped tarragon.*

2 *Using a spoon, shape the egg mixture into 8 quenelles (balls) and poach them in barely simmering salted water for about 3 minutes. Drain on a clean kitchen towel.*

3 *Blanch the peas in salted water, drain, and refresh.*

4 *Slice the mushrooms in half. Melt the knob of butter in a frying pan and sauté the mushrooms. When nearly cooked, add the lemon juice, garlic, salt and pepper. Add the tomato, parsley, 1 teaspoon chives, peas, and fava beans, stir, then add the crème fraîche and bring to a boil. Once the sauce is boiling, remove from the heat.*

5 *Meanwhile, make the sabayon. Mix all the ingredients together in a cup and add 3 tablespoons of the cooking liquor from the mushrooms.*

To serve: *Spoon the mushroom ragout into 4 soup plates and place 2 quenelles on top. Spoon over the sabayon sauce, sprinkle the chives on top and serve immediately.*

Wild Morel Tamale with Pico de Gallo & Cilantro Oil

Ingredients

serves 4

1 ear corn

3 tbsp butter

1¹/₂ tbsp chopped fresh cilantro (coriander)

3 cloves garlic, roasted, peeled & chopped

¹/₂ cup (4 oz/125 g) lard

pinch salt

³/₄ tsp baking powder

1 tbsp chopped canned chipotle chilies

1¹/₂ tbsp powdered wild mushrooms (buy ready-made, or grind dried morels or porcini in a spice mill)

³/₄ cup (4 oz/125 g) masa harina

¹/₂ cup (4 fl oz/125 ml) chicken or vegetable stock

4 large dried corn husks, soaked in warm water until soft

¹/₂ cup (¹/₂ oz/15 g) morels (plus a few for garnish), soaked (liquid reserved) & rinsed

¹/₂ tbsp vegetable oil

for the cilantro oil

2 cups fresh cilantro (coriander), blanched & squeezed dry

¹/₂ cup (4 fl oz/125 ml) vegetable oil

¹/₂ cup (4 fl oz/125 ml) olive oil

METHOD

1 *Roast the corn in a 400°F (200°C) oven for 15 minutes. Leave to cool, then cut off the kernels. Meanwhile, mix the butter, cilantro, and 2 garlic cloves and set aside. Whirl the ingredients for the cilantro oil in a blender for 5–6 minutes to form a smooth green purée. Set aside.*

2 *Whip the lard with a pinch of salt, the baking powder, chipotles, and mushroom powder. Mix the masa harina and chicken stock, and gradually add to the lard, beating for 10–15 minutes until light and fluffy. Fold in the corn.*

3 *Place equal portions of dough in the center of each of the 4 corn husks and wrap the husks completely over, twisting the ends and securing with husks or string. Steam for 30–40 minutes, seam side down.*

4 *Meanwhile, roughly chop the morels and sauté them in vegetable oil. Pass the reserved mushroom liquid through a very fine sieve or tea towel to remove any grit and add to the pan. Add remaining garlic and cook until all the liquid has evaporated. Leave to cool slightly, then stir in the butter mixture, a little at a time. Set aside and keep warm.*

To serve: *When the tamales are cooked, lay 1 on each plate. Make a small lengthwise slit down the middle, then push both ends together to open up as you would a baked potato. Pour some morel sauce over the top, garnish with pico de gallo, and drizzle with cilantro oil.*

Pico de Gallo

METHOD

1 *Place the onion in a sieve and run hot water over them for about 5 minutes, then drain.*

2 *Meanwhile, blanch, skin, and seed the plum tomatoes. Dice and place into a bowl. Add the onion and the remaining ingredients and mix together.*

3 *Season to taste and allow to sit for at least 30 minutes before using, so that the flavors intensify.*

Ingredients

1 tbsp diced onion

3 plum (Roma) tomatoes

1 small jalapeno chili, chopped

1 tbsp chopped, fresh cilantro (coriander)

1 tbsp sugar

1 tbsp olive oil

lime juice to taste

pinch salt

Monkfish, Clams, Samphire & Trompettes de la Mort

METHOD

1 *Clean and scrub the clams and set aside. Blanch the samphire in boiling water for 15 seconds and then refresh in ice water, drain, and set aside. Sauté the mushrooms lightly in ¹/₂ tablespoon of the oil for 20–30 seconds, season with salt and pepper, and drain on paper towels.*

2 *Meanwhile, make the butter sauce. In a deep saucepan, heat the oil and sweat the shallots. When they are soft, deglaze with the white wine vinegar, add the white wine, and cook until the liquid is reduced by half. Add the butter and whisk in to form an emulsion. Remove from the heat, pass through a tea towel or fine sieve, and set aside.*

3 *Season the monkfish portions with salt and pepper. Place ¹/₂ tablespoon of oil in a hot frying pan and sear the monkfish pieces until they are golden. Transfer to a baking dish and place in a 400°F (200°C) oven for 4 minutes.*

4 *While the fish is cooking, place ¹/₂ tablespoon of the oil in a hot pan and sauté the clams. Add the wine and place a lid on the pan to steam open the clams. When the clams are open, add the samphire, mushrooms, and tomato, and toss together. Then pour in the butter sauce, mix well, and remove from the heat.*

To serve: *Spoon the clam mixture into 4 bowls. Slice each of the monkfish pieces into 4 slivers and fan across the top of each serving.*

Ingredients

serves 4

20 small clams

10 oz (315 g) salicornia, or other wild mushroom

10 oz (315 g) trompette de la mort mushrooms

1¹/₂ tbsp vegetable oil

salt & pepper

about 8 oz (250 g) monkfish fillet, cut into 4 pieces

4 tbsp (2 fl oz/60 ml) white wine

10 oz (315 g) tomatoes, seeded & diced

for the butter sauce

¹/₂ tbsp vegetable oil

2 shallots, sliced

2 tbsp white wine vinegar

scant 1 cup (7 fl oz/220 ml) dry white wine

²/₃ cup (5 oz/155 g) butter, diced

Squab, Wild Mushroom & Barolo Risotto

Ingredients

serves 4

1 squab (pigeon) (7 oz/220 g), diced

1 cup (8 fl oz/250 ml) Barolo wine

2 onions, thinly sliced

1 carrot, peeled & diced

1 celery stalk, finely diced

1 fresh thyme sprig

1 fresh rosemary sprig

1 bay leaf

1 tbsp vegetable oil

2 oz (60 g) porcini mushrooms (cèpes), diced

1 oz (30 g) speck, diced

2 cups (16 fl oz/500 ml) game stock

salt & pepper

1 clove garlic

$^{1}/_{2}$ tbsp olive oil

1$^{2}/_{3}$ cups (10 oz/315 g) Arboro rice

scant 1 cup (7 fl oz/220 ml) white wine

3 qt (3 l) vegetable stock

6–7 oz (185–220 g) mixed wild mushrooms

4 tbsp (2 oz/60 g) fois gras butter (from good delicatessens)

METHOD

1 *Two days in advance, marinate the squab in the Barolo wine, 1 onion, carrot, celery, and herbs.*

2 *Heat $^{1}/_{2}$ tablespoon of the vegetable oil in a heavy pan and lightly sauté the porcini and speck.*

3 *Remove the squab from the marinade (reserve the marinade) and add to the pan, sautéing for a couple of minutes.*

4 *Now add the marinade and cook until reduced. Then add the game stock and simmer slowly until it reduces to a thick ragout. Check the seasoning and set aside.*

5 *Sauté the remaining onion and the garlic in the olive oil, then add the rice. Sauté for a couple of minutes, add the white wine and cook until reduced. Add the vegetable stock and cook the rice until almost done, about 20 minutes.*

6 *Meanwhile, sauté the wild mushrooms in the remaining $^{1}/_{2}$ tablespoon vegetable oil and season well. Add the ragout to the rice and cook for a further 5 minutes. Finally add the fois gras butter and mix in. Remove from the heat.*

To serve: *Check seasoning and serve immediately.*

Pork Sausage with Purée of Caramelized Cauliflower

METHOD

1 *Soak the pig's feet in water for 24 hours. Drain and peel off skin. Put the sugar in a large saucepan and cook over low heat until it caramelizes. Add the feet and cook for a further 5 minutes. Add enough cold water to just cover the feet, then bring to a boil and skim. Turn down the heat to simmer and add the diced pork shoulder. Skim again after a few minutes and add the vegetables, bouquet garni, cloves, quatre épices, salt, and pepper. Simmer for 3 hours.*

2 *Meanwhile, make the duxelles. Finely chop the button mushrooms. Melt a knob of butter in a frying pan and sweat the shallots until soft. Add the mushrooms and Madeira and cook until the liquid evaporates. Set aside.*

3 *When the pork feet and shoulder are tender, remove from the pot, strain the liquid, and reserve. Discard the vegetables.*

4 *Place a third of the braising liquid back in the pot and bring to a boil. Lower the heat and simmer until reduced to a syrup. Meanwhile, make the stuffing in a bowl, mixing the shoulder, duxelles, rillettes, egg white, thyme leaves, and cognac. Season. Add the reduced syrup from the pot.*

Recipe continued overleaf...

Ingredients

serves 4

4 pig's feet

4 tbsp (2 oz/60 g) sugar

about 7 oz (200 g) pork shoulder, diced

1 carrot, peeled & chopped

1 onion, chopped

1 celery stalk, chopped

1 leek, chopped

1 bouquet garni

3 whole cloves

pinch quatre épices

salt & pepper

4 oz (125 g) pork rillettes

1 egg white, beaten stiff

leaves from 1 thyme sprig

1 tbsp good cognac

4 oz (125 g) caul fat, soaked for 24 hours to remove blood

for the duxelles

4 oz (125 g) button mushrooms

knob of butter

2 shallots, chopped

4 tbsp (2 fl oz/60 ml) Madeira wine

Ingredients

for the purée of

caramelized cauliflower

1 large cauliflower

$^{1}/_{2}$ cup (4 oz/125 g) unsalted
butter

knob of butter

2 tbsp milk

salt & pepper

Recipe continued from previous page...

5 *Scrape the inside of the feet to remove membrane. Then place skin side down on a work surface and fill with stuffing. Wrap each foot into a tight sausage shape using plastic wrap and refrigerate. When chilled, remove plastic wrap.*

6 *On a chopping board, cut the caul fat into 4 rectangles, each about 8 by 5 inches (20 by 13 cm). Place a foot at the base of each rectangle and roll up to form a sausage. Braise the sausages in a 300°F (150°C) oven for 30 minutes, basting regularly with the reserved cooking liquor.*

To serve: *Serve each sausage with cauliflower purée (see recipe below), blanched baby vegetables, and sautéed porcini (cèpes).*

Purée of Caramelized Cauliflower

METHOD

1 *Remove the cauliflower stems and chop the head into small florets. Heat the butter in a pan over the lowest heat and add the cauliflower pieces. Sauté gently for about 40 minutes, or until very soft.*

2 *Remove the cauliflower pieces from the pan, draining off the butter, and place in a blender. Add a knob of butter, the milk, salt, and pepper. Blend until smooth.*

3 *Pour through a sieve to remove any remaining lumps, and keep warm until ready to serve.*

Roast Lamb with Wild Mushroom Hash Browns

METHOD

1 *Prepare the mushroom duxelles in advance.*

2 *Preheat the oven to 350°F (180°C). Remove the eye of the meat from the bones and trim off any excess fat. Chop the bones and trimmings and reserve.*

3 *Peel and chop the carrot, onion, and celery.*

4 *Place the bones, trimmings, chopped vegetables, and bay leaves on a baking sheet (tray) and bake in a 350°F (180°C) oven until golden brown, around 30 minutes.*

5 *When done, transfer to a pot, leaving any fats behind. Add the water and the veal stock, bring to a boil, skim, then simmer for 45 minutes.*

6 *Cut the eggplant into 12 rounds, sprinkle with salt and lay on paper towels to drain. Meanwhile, peel and grate the potatoes, then wrap in a kitchen towel and squeeze out excess water.*

Recipe continued overleaf...

Ingredients

serves 4

1 recipe wild mushroom duxelles (see recipe page 152)

3 single racks of lamb

1 carrot

1 onion

2 celery stalks

2 bay leaves

2 qt (2 l) water

3 cups (24 fl oz/750 ml) veal stock

1 medium eggplant (aubergine)

salt & pepper

4 large potatoes

4 1/2 tbsp (2 1/4 fl oz/70 ml) sunflower oil

2 fresh rosemary sprigs, leaves removed & chopped

12 cloves garlic, peeled

4 fresh rosemary sprigs, for garnish

Recipe continued from previous page...

7 *Heat 2 tablespoons of the oil in a large ovenproof frying pan, add half of the grated potato, and push down to cover the bottom of the pan. Season with a little salt and pepper. Spread the duxelles over the top. You do not need to use all the duxelles, just enough to cover the surface of the potato. Place the remaining grated potato on top, season and cook for about 10 minutes, or until the bottom is golden.*

8 *Carefully turn the potato "cake" and cook again for 10 minutes, or until the other side is golden, then remove from the stove top. Bake in a 375°F (190°C) oven for about 25 minutes, or until cooked through. Set aside.*

9 *By now the lamb stock should be ready. Pass through a fine sieve, return to the pot and gently reduce over low to medium heat, skimming as often as possible. Reduce until you have about 1¼ cups (10 fl oz/310 ml) of a good sauce consistency. Pass once more through the sieve and set aside.*

10 *Season the lamb with salt, pepper and the chopped rosemary. Heat ½ tablespoon of the oil in an ovenproof frying pan, and sear the lamb on one side until golden, about 3 minutes. Turn the lamb over and repeat.*

11 *Add the garlic to the pan, then place in the oven, again preheated to 350°F (180°C), for about 10 minutes, or until the meat is medium rare.*

12 *Remove the lamb from the pan, place on a rack, cover to keep warm, and allow to rest. Drop the garlic cloves into the reserved sauce.*

13 *Meanwhile, wipe out the pan and heat 2 tablespoons of oil. Pat the eggplant dry, then sauté in batches until golden brown. Set aside and keep warm.*

14 *When ready to serve, cut the potato cake into portions, but not so big as to dwarf the meat, and warm in the oven for a few minutes, along with the lamb and eggplant. Reheat the sauce gently in a saucepan.*

15 *When the lamb is warmed, cut into 12 steaks.*

To serve: *Lay 3 slices of eggplant, just overlapping, in the center of each plate. Place 3 slices of lamb on top so they are sitting upright, with pink side facing out, using a sprig of rosemary as the central support. Pour a little sauce over the top and around. Rest a wedge of the potato against the lamb. Decorate each plate with a few of the cooked garlic cloves.*

Ingredients

serves 4

1 cup (3 oz/90 g) leek, diced

³/₄ cup (3 oz/90 g) celery, diced

³/₄ cup (3 oz/90 g) carrot, diced

2 knobs of butter

²/₃ cup dried white beans, soaked overnight

4 cod steaks, 5 oz (155 g) each

¹/₂ cup (4 fl oz/125 ml) heavy (double) cream

¹/₂ cup (4 fl oz/125 ml) heavy cream, whipped

salt & pepper

2 shallots, sliced

about 7 oz (220 g) chanterelle (girolle) mushrooms

¹/₂ cup (3 oz/90 g) diced tomato

12 large shrimp (prawns), cooked & peeled

for the shrimp stock

shells reserved from cooked shrimp

1 carrot, diced

1 onion, diced

1 celery stalk, diced

4 cups (32 fl oz/1 l) mushroom stock

1 tbsp chopped fresh parsley

1 tbsp chopped fresh thyme

Roast Cod with a Casserole of Shrimp, White Beans & Mushroom Sauce

METHOD

1 *Place the ingredients for the stock into a large saucepan. Simmer for 1 hour to reduce to 2 cups (16 fl oz/500 ml).*

2 *In another pan, sweat the diced leek, celery, and carrot in a knob of butter. Add the beans and cover with a little stock. Cook gently for 45 minutes, or until the beans are tender.*

3 *Sear the cod in a very hot ovenproof pan for about 20 seconds on each side. Finish cooking in a 350°F (180°C) oven for about 7 minutes.*

4 *Bring the stock to a boil, then lower the heat. Add heavy cream and simmer for 5–7 minutes until reduced. Finish by adding the whipped cream and quickly bringing to a boil. Remove from the heat and process in a blender until light and frothy. Add salt and pepper to taste.*

5 *Melt the remaining knob of butter in a pan and sauté the shallots, mushrooms, and tomato for a few minutes until soft.*

To serve: *Place a bed of white beans in the center of each plate.*

Top with a piece of the roast cod, along with a portion of the mushrooms.

Arrange the cooked shrimp around the outside and drizzle with the sauce.

Crepinette of Scallops, Spinach & Porcini with Velouté of Fava Beans & Morels

METHOD

1 *Shuck the scallops, removing the meat and the skirt that runs around the edge of each shell. Wash and pat dry. Slice each scallop into 5 disks and very lightly coat with half the oil. Set aside, along with the skirts.*

2 *Melt half of the butter in a hot pan and cook the baby spinach. Season with salt and pepper and add nutmeg. Set aside.*

3 *If using fresh porcini, blanch for 2 minutes and dry. Cut off caps and reserve. Slice each base into 6 pieces and lightly sauté on each side in the remaining oil. Reserve.*

4 *Cut the cardboard core of a paper towel roll down to a length of about 3 inches (7.5 cm). Line with plastic wrap so that the it forms a pouch inside, with the ends protruding from the top of the roll. Assemble the crepinettes by alternating layers of the scallops, porcini, and spinach. Start with a slice of scallop, lowering it into the roll so that it is suspended*

at the bottom of the plastic wrap. Continue the layering, starting and finishing with the scallops and allowing 3 slices of porcini per crepinette. As each one is assembled, ease it out of the roll, gently pulling the ends of the wrap and pushing up the pouch to reveal a small cylinder of the layered ingredients. Wrap in plastic wrap and refrigerate for 2 hours until firm.

5 *When firm, unwrap and then wrap each crepinette in a rectangle of caul fat about 5 by 6 inches (12 by 15 cm). Set aside until just prior to serving.*

6 *To make the velouté, sweat the scallop skirts in a third of the butter for 5 minutes. Add the stock or water and savory or thyme, and bring to a boil. Lower the heat and simmer for 30 minutes. Strain and reserve the stock.*

7 *Sweat the shallots, garlic, and porcini caps (reserved from crepinette) in another third of the butter for 5 minutes. Add white wine and vermouth and cook to reduce. Add the scallop stock and simmer for 15 minutes. Add two-thirds of the fava beans and the cream, and boil for 5 minutes. Transfer to a blender, purée, and pass through a fine sieve. Keep warm.*

8 *Sauté the morels and the rest of the fava beans in the rest of the butter, 1 tablespoon of the water, salt, and pepper.*

9 *Brown the crepinettes in butter in an ovenproof pan, add a little water, and braise in a 300°F (150°C) oven for 3 minutes.*

To serve: *Place a crepinette in the center of each plate and pour the velouté around it. Garnish with the morels and fava beans.*

Ingredients

serves *4*

for the crepinette

4 large sea scallops in the shell

1 tbsp olive oil

4 tbsp (2 oz/60 g) unsalted butter

4 oz (125 g) baby spinach

salt & pepper

pinch of ground nutmeg

2 medium fresh or frozen porcini (cèpe) mushrooms

4 oz (125 g) caul fat, soaked for 24 hours to remove blood

for the velouté

$^1/_2$ cup (4 oz/125 g) butter

1 cup (7 fl oz/220 ml) fish stock or water, plus 2 tbsp water

1 bunch winter savory or thyme

4 shallots, finely chopped

$^1/_2$ clove garlic, finely chopped

$^2/_3$ cup (5 fl oz/150 ml) dry white wine

4 tbsp (2 fl oz/60 ml) vermouth

12 oz (375 g) shelled fava (broad) beans, blanched & peeled

4 tbsp (2 fl oz/60 ml) heavy (double) cream

2 oz (60 g) fresh or dried baby morel mushrooms (if dried, soak & rinse well)

Carpaccio of Beef, Bruschetta & Wild Mushrooms

Ingredients

serves 2

2 filets mignons, 4 oz (125 g) each

salt & pepper

5 tbsp olive oil

4 slices ciabatta or other coarse country bread, each 1/4 inch (6 mm) thick

5 oz (155 g) mixed wild mushrooms

4 oz (125 g) mixed salad greens

1 oz (30 g) Parmesan cheese, cut into shavings (optional)

for the salad dressing

1/2 tsp Dijon mustard

2 tbsp olive oil

2 tbsp sunflower oil

pinch pepper

pinch salt

4 tbsp (2 fl oz/60 ml) Cabernet Sauvignon vinegar or other red wine vinegar

METHOD

1 *Prepare the salad dressing in advance, blending all the ingredients together. Set aside.*

2 *Season the steaks with salt and pepper and sear in a hot, lightly oiled pan, leaving the beef in for just long enough to color the outside. Remove from the pan and let cool.*

3 *Meanwhile, make the bruschetta. Dip the bread slices into olive oil and bake in a 300°F (150°C) oven until pale gold.*

4 *While the bread is baking, heat 1 tablespoon of the olive oil in a pan and sauté the mushrooms until they have absorbed the oil and are moist. Remove from the pan.*

5 *Dress the salad. The bruschetta should now be ready. Remove from the oven and leave to cool for a few minutes.*

To serve: *Place a mound of salad on each slice of bruschetta and place a steak over it. Arrange the mushrooms on top, drizzle with a little more dressing and serve. Finish with shavings of Parmesan, if desired.*

Lasagna of Shrimp, Pig's Feet & Truffles

METHOD

1 *Sauté the beans in the butter and a pinch of salt until soft, then transfer to a blender and blend to a purée.*

2 *Roll out the pasta dough into 12 thin sheets, each 6 by 4 inches (15 by 10 cm). Blanch, refresh and reserve.*

3 *Pour the cream into a saucepan, bring to a boil and cook to reduce by two-thirds. Add the carrots, boil for 1 minute, then add the duxelles, bean purée and minced truffle. Boil for 1 minute, remove from heat, season, and add lemon juice.*

4 *Place 1 sheet of pasta on a work surface. Spread with the vegetable mix, sprinkle with the shredded meat, and place 2 shrimp on top. Place another sheet of pasta over this and repeat, this time using 1 shrimp and 1 slice of truffle. Place the third sheet of pasta on top. Continue with the process until you have made 4 lasagnas.*

5 *For the sauce, bring truffle juice, chicken stock, and leeks to a boil and cook to reduce by one-third. Stir in the truffle and butter, and finish with a squeeze of lemon juice. Keep warm.*

6 *Steam the lasagnas over boiling water for 6–8 minutes, or until cooked.*

To serve: *Pour the sauce over each lasagna and garnish with chervil.*

Ingredients

serves 4

for the lasagna

4 oz (125 g) haricots verts or other slender green beans, blanched & refreshed

knob of butter

salt & pepper

4 oz (125 g) pasta dough

$^1/_2$ cup (4 fl oz/125 ml) heavy (double) cream

4 oz (125 g) carrots, peeled & diced into tiny cubes

$^1/_4$ recipe mushroom duxelles (see recipe page 152)

1 oz (30 g) truffle, minced, plus 4 thin slices

juice of $^1/_2$ lemon

about $^1/_2$ cup shredded meat from braised pig feet

12 medium shrimp (prawns), cooked & peeled

$^1/_2$ bunch fresh chervil for garnish

for the sauce

4 tbsp (2 fl oz/60 ml) truffle juice

4 tbsp (2 fl oz/60 ml) chicken stock

$^1/_3$ cup (1 oz/30 g) chopped leek, white part only

slice of truffle, julienned

1 tsp cold butter

juice of $^1/_2$ lemon

Millefeuille of Salmon, Leek & Seasonal Wild Mushrooms

METHOD

1 *Prepare the wild mushrooms, brushing off any dirt and discarding stems. Lightly sauté in 1 tablespoon of the extra-virgin olive oil, making sure all are cooked. Season with salt and pepper, remove from the pan, and drain on paper towels.*

2 *Wash leeks well and cut white and pale green parts only into slices about 1 ½ inches (4 cm) thick. Lightly sauté in a pan with 1 tablespoon of the extra-virgin olive oil.*

3 *Peel the parsnips, then cut into shavings with a vegetable peeler. Deep-fry in oil at 350°F (180°C) until golden brown. Remove and drain on paper towels.*

4 *Cut each piece of salmon lengthwise into 3 strips. Heat the 1 tablespoon vegetable oil in a pan and sauté the salmon strips very lightly (about 1 minute each side). Remove from pan and drain on paper towels.*

To serve: *On each serving plate, layer a strip of salmon topped by a sautéed leek, followed by the wild mushrooms. Repeat and place the third strip of salmon on top. Finish with the deep-fried shaved parsnip. Lightly drizzle with the remaining 6 tablespoons (3 fl oz/90 ml) olive oil and the balsamic vinegar.*

Ingredients

serves 4

1½ lb (750 g) mixed wild mushrooms

½ cup (4 fl oz/125 ml) extra-virgin olive oil

salt & pepper

2 leeks

2 medium parsnips

4 cups (32 fl oz/1 l) vegetable oil for deep-frying, plus 1 tbsp

4 salmon fillets, 5 oz (155 g) each

4 tbsp (2 fl oz/60 ml) good-quality balsamic vinegar

Wild Mushrooms on Thyme Rösti with Leek Sprouts & Sour Cream

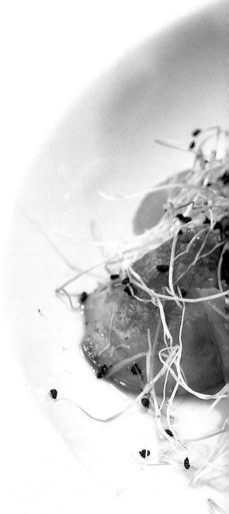

Ingredients

serves 4

2 large new potatoes

salt & pepper

4 tbsp (2 oz/60 g) butter, softened

1¹/₃ cups (2 oz/60 g) chopped fresh thyme

4 tbsp (2 fl oz/60 ml) vegetable oil

1 lb (500 g) wild mushrooms

1 tbsp extra-virgin olive oil

4 green (spring) onions, chopped

4 oz (125 g) wild garlic leaves

2 tomatoes

1¹/₃ cups (10 fl oz/310 ml) sour cream

4 oz (125 g) leek sprouts (or other sprouts if unavailable)

METHOD

1 *Wash, peel, and grate the potatoes. Season with salt and leave to sit for a few minutes. Then wrap them in a kitchen towel and squeeze out the excess water.*

2 *Mix the butter and the thyme into the grated potato and form into 4 patties. Shallow-fry on both sides in the vegetable oil until golden brown and crisp. Remove from the pan and drain.*

3 *Clean the wild mushrooms and sauté in a frying pan with the olive oil. Add the green onions and wild garlic leaves and season. Remove from the heat.*

4 *Peel, quarter, and seed the tomatoes, and cut each quarter into 4 strips.*

To serve: *Place a portion of the fried potato on each dish and arrange the mushrooms on top. Spoon a dollop of sour cream onto the mushrooms. Arrange several tomato strips around and finish with a sprinkling of leek sprouts.*

Herb Tagliatelle with Baby Clams, Garlic & Porcini Mushrooms

METHOD

1 *Heat the olive oil in a frying pan over medium heat and fry the garlic until it is golden brown, then remove.*

2 *Add the baby clams and shallots, and cover until the clams open.*

3 *Place the sliced porcini mushrooms in the pan and sauté until soft, then add the wine. Let simmer gently for 5 minutes while you cook the pasta.*

4 *Cook the tagliatelle in a large pan of salted boiling water until al dente, about 2–3 minutes, and drain.*

5 *Add the pasta to the other ingredients and toss.*

To serve: *Garnish with the parsley and diced tomato.*

Ingredients

serves 4

3 tbsp olive oil

5 cloves garlic, crushed

8 oz (250 g) baby clams

4 shallots, chopped

10 oz (315 g) porcini (cèpe) mushrooms, sliced

³/₄ cup (6 fl oz/180 ml) white wine

10 oz (315 g) fresh herb tagliatelle

pinch salt

¹/₂ bunch fresh flat-leaf parsley, chopped

2 tbsp diced plum (Roma) tomato

Ingredients

serves 4

4 slices ciabatta or other coarse country bread

1 clove garlic

4 tbsp (2 fl oz/60 ml) olive oil

2 tbsp sea salt

$^1/_3$ cup (2 oz/60 g) chopped shallots

6–7 oz (185–220 g) chanterelle (girolle) mushrooms

scant 1 cup (7 fl oz/220 ml) white wine vinegar

pepper to taste

4 eggs

6–7 oz (185–220 g) arugula (rocket) leaves

for the pesto

2 cups (10 oz/280 g) loosely packed fresh basil leaves

$^1/_3$ cup (1 oz/30 g) pine nuts

2 medium cloves garlic, chopped

$^1/_2$ cup (2 oz/60 g) grated Parmesan cheese

$^1/_2$ cup (4 fl oz/120 ml) olive oil

$^1/_2$ teaspoon salt

Crostini with Chanterelles, Poached Egg & Pesto Dressing

METHOD

1 *Make the pesto puréeing all the ingredients in a blender or mortar, or use a ready-made pesto, if preferred.*

2 *You can make the crostini in advance. Rub each slice of bread with the clove of garlic, drizzle with 3 tablespoons of the olive oil, sprinkle with a little of the sea salt, and place in the oven on a baking sheet (tray). Bake at 350°F (180°C) until golden, about 20 minutes.*

3 *Ten minutes before you are ready to serve, reheat the crostini in a low oven. While they are warming, gently heat the remaining tablespoon olive oil in a frying pan and add the shallots. Sweat them until they lose their color.*

4 *Turn up the heat and sauté the chanterelles. Add 2 table-spoons white wine vinegar, season with sea salt and pepper, and sauté for a final minute. Then remove from the heat.*

5 *Meanwhile, poach the eggs in boiling water, mixed with the remaining white wine vinegar, for around 3 minutes.*

To serve: *Place the mushrooms and a poached egg on a base of arugula leaves, with the crostini to the side. Drizzle liberally with pesto. Reserve any remaining pesto for another use.*

Roasted Porcini Feuillentine

METHOD

1 *Cut the filo pastry sheets into twelve 8-inch (20-cm) squares. Reserve remaining filo for another use.*

2 *To make each tart, stack 3 filo squares, positioning them at 45-degree angles to one another, and brush each with clarified butter.*

3 *Fold the edges over to form a round tart base. Set aside.*

4 *Heat a large frying pan and add most of the olive oil. Sauté the mushrooms, shallots, and garlic until golden brown. Drain the mushrooms on a paper towels and transfer to a mixing bowl. Season and add the parsley and chives.*

5 *Place some of the mushroom mixture into each tart, drizzle a little olive oil over, and sprinkle with the Parmesan cheese. Place the tarts on a nonstick baking sheet (tray) and cook in a preheated 350°F (180°C) oven for 8–10 minutes, or until the base of the tart is golden brown.*

To serve: *Place a still-warm tart on each plate and serve with a salad of mixed greens on the side.*

Ingredients

serves 4

1 package of filo pastry

1³/₄ cups (7 oz/220 g) unsalted clarified butter, melted

scant 1 cup (7 fl oz/220 ml) olive oil

1¹/₄ lb (625 g) fresh or frozen porcini (cèpe) mushrooms, cut into quarters

3 shallots, thinly sliced

2 cloves garlic, finely chopped

salt & white pepper

¹/₂ bunch fresh flat-leaf parsley, blanched, refreshed & finely chopped

¹/₂ bunch fresh chives, finely chopped

1 cup (4 oz/125 g) grated Parmesan cheese

Roast Rabbit Leg with Olives, Thyme & Portobello Mushrooms

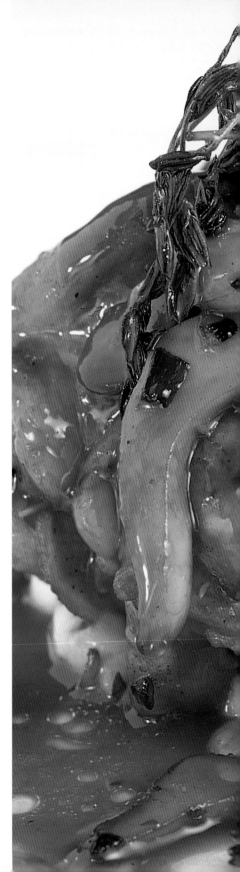

Ingredients

serves 4

4 rabbit legs, boned

4 cloves garlic

4 oz (125 g) butter, cut into 4 equal cubes

1 lb (500 g) mixed mirepoix vegetables (carrot, onion, celery & leek), chopped

2 cups (16 fl oz/500 ml) chicken stock

1 tbsp olive oil

4 oz (125 g) shallots, chopped

²/₃ cup (3 oz/90 g) pitted black olives

2 fresh thyme sprigs

about 1 cup (4 oz/125 g) shelled, blanched & peeled fava (broad) beans

4 oz (125g) portobello or other large flat mushrooms, sliced

8 large potatoes, peeled

knob of butter

2 tbsp chopped mixed fresh herbs

METHOD

1 *Place a garlic clove and butter cube inside the cavity of each rabbit leg. Sear in a large saucepan.*

2 *Remove the rabbit pieces from the pan, turn off the heat, and place the mirepoix vegetables in the bottom of the pan. Place the rabbit pieces on top, pour in the chicken stock, and cover. Braise over low heat until done, about 1 hour.*

3 *Heat the oil in a pan, add the chopped shallots, and sweat until soft. Add the black olives, thyme sprig, broad beans, and portobello mushrooms and sweat until cooked. Meanwhile, boil the potatoes vigorously, then drain and mash, stirring in a little butter and the chopped herbs.*

To serve: *Place a bed of mashed potato on each plate and top with a rabbit leg. Cover with the mushroom and olive mixture and spoon some of the juices from the cooked rabbit around the plate.*

Saucisson de Foie Gras & Champignons Sauvages

METHOD

1 *Clean the foie gras and refrigerate until needed.*

2 *Melt the butter in a frying pan and sauté the shallots for about a minute, then add the mushrooms and cook for another 5 minutes, stirring regularly.*

3 *Add the cream and bring to a boil. Then add the gelatin and lower the heat, stirring well for a further minute. Remove from the heat.*

4 *Reserve the mixture in the refrigerator. When cold, turn it out onto a chopping board and roll it into a sausage.*

5 *Remove the foie gras from the refrigerator and lay it out flat on the board. Place the sausage at the base of the foie gras and roll up. Wrap tightly in plastic wrap.*

6 *Bring a pan of water to a boil. Place the roll, still wrapped in plastic wrap, in the pan and reduce the heat. Simmer gently for 20 minutes. Remove from the water and allow to cool slightly before removing the plastic wrap and cutting the roll into even slices.*

To serve: *Serve by the slice with a portion of mixed salad greens.*

Ingredients

serves 4

4 oz (125 g) raw foie gras

knob of butter

2 shallots, finely chopped

6–7 oz (185–220 g) mixed wild mushrooms, sliced

$1/2$ cup (4 fl oz/125 ml) heavy (double) cream

$1/8$ oz (2 g) leaf gelatin, dissolved in 1 cup (8 fl oz/ 250 ml) hot water, or $1^{1}/_{2}$ tsp powdered gelatin, softened in a few tbsp cold water for 3–5 minutes, then dissolved in the 1 cup hot water

mixed salad greens for garnish

Risotto of Foie Gras & Truffles

METHOD

1 *Trim the celery and cut into 1-inch (2.5-cm) batons. Blanch in salted water for a few seconds.*

2 *Slice the truffle, not too thinly, and combine in a mixing bowl with the celery. Season with salt, pepper, 1 tablespoon of the olive oil, and the red wine vinegar. Leave to marinate for an hour before serving.*

3 *Heat a tablespoon of the olive oil in a frying pan, add the onion, and sweat for 2–3 minutes, or until translucent but not browned. Add the rice and continue to cook for a further 6 minutes.*

4 *Add enough chicken stock to cover and cook, stirring often and adding more chicken stock as the liquid is absorbed, for about 25 minutes. The finished rice should be loose but not swimming in the stock. Remove from the heat.*

5 *Season the rice and stir in the mascarpone and truffle oil. The cheese should melt slightly on contact with the rice.*

6 *Quickly heat the remaining olive oil in a pan and lightly sauté the foie gras slices. Remove from the heat and serve immediately with the risotto.*

To serve: *Arrange the pan-fried foie gras over each plate of risotto, and spoon the reserved truffle and celery salad on top.*

Ingredients

serves 4

2 celery stalks

1 1/2 oz (45 g) fresh truffle

salt & pepper

2 1/4 tbsp olive oil

1 tbsp red wine vinegar

1 large onion, finely chopped

1 3/4 cups (11 oz/330 g) Arborio rice

3 cups (24 fl oz/750 ml) chicken stock

7 oz (220 g) mascarpone cheese

2 tbsp truffle oil

3 oz (90 g) raw foie gras, sliced

Ingredients

serves 4

4 tbsp peanut (groundnut) oil

1 lb (500 g) mixed mushrooms such as portobello, oyster, and morel

salt & pepper

4 eggs

1 tbsp white wine vinegar

6 shallots, finely diced

2 cloves garlic, chopped

1 black truffle, precooked, peeled, and finely diced

1 tbsp chopped fresh chervil

Note: Black truffles can be bought ready-cooked and peeled.

Ragout of Mushrooms, Warm Poached Eggs & Black Truffles

METHOD

1 *Heat a tablespoon of peanut oil in a pan and sauté each type of mushroom separately. Season, adding more of the oil as needed. Remove each batch from the pan and keep warm.*

2 *Poach the eggs in water mixed with the vinegar for 3–4 minutes, making sure the yolks are soft.*

3 *Heat a little more oil in a pan and sweat the shallots and garlic. Mix with the mushrooms.*

To serve: *Arrange a mound of mushrooms on each serving dish, place a poached egg on top, and finish with diced black truffle and a sprinkling of chervil.*

Paris Mushroom, Fennel & Parmesan Salad

METHOD

1 *Trim the fennel bulbs and cut into very thin slices. Place in iced lemon water to keep them crisp and prevent discoloring. Clean the mushrooms, discarding the stalks, and slice them thinly. Chop the chives.*

2 *To make the dressing, squeeze the lemons into a bowl and add the crushed garlic, seasoning, and a pinch of sugar. Whisk until blended. Taste to check it is not too sour, adding sugar as necessary. Gradually whisk in the peanut oil, using just enough to soften, but not cover, the intense lemony taste.*

3 *When ready to serve, drain the fennel and blot dry with paper towels. Mix together with the mushrooms and chives and dressing in a bowl.*

To serve: *Arrange the salad in small mounds on each plate and sprinkle a few Parmesan shavings on top. Serve with crusty bread.*

Ingredients

serves 4

2 fennel bulbs

bowl of iced lemon water

8 oz (250 g) button mushrooms

1 small bunch fresh chives

2 lemons

1 clove garlic, crushed

salt & pepper

pinch sugar

$^2/_3$ cup (5 fl oz/150 ml) peanut (groundnut) oil

Parmesan cheese shavings

Giant Portobello Mushrooms with Artichoke Stew

METHOD

1 *Pare down the artichoke heads to hearts by cutting off the stems, breaking off the leaves all the way down to the choke, and removing the choke. Leave the hearts in the iced lemon water to prevent discoloring.*

2 *Clean the mushrooms and remove the stems. Place on a baking sheet (tray) and dress with 2 tablespoons of the olive oil, salt, and pepper. Roast in a 400°F (200°C) oven for 15 minutes, or until soft. Remove from the oven and keep warm.*

3 *While the mushrooms are roasting, heat 2 tablespoons of the olive oil in a frying pan over medium heat and add the shallots. When they are soft but not brown, add the chili, garlic, and a pinch of salt.*

4 *Thickly slice the artichoke hearts and add to the pan. Cook for a few minutes, turning the contents of the pan constantly, and add just enough cold water to cover the mixture. Continue to cook for about 15 minutes, or until the water has nearly gone and the artichokes are cooked through. If they are not ready, add a bit more water and cook further. Check seasoning and remove from heat.*

5 *Mix the artichoke mixture with the arugula leaves.*

To serve: *Arrange a mound of the artichoke-arugula mix on each plate. Top with the warm portobello mushrooms and drizzle over any remaining liquid from the pan.*

Ingredients

serves 4

2 large artichokes

bowl of iced lemon water

4 large portobello mushrooms

4 tbsp (2 fl oz/60 ml) olive oil

salt & pepper

2 shallots, finely chopped

pinch of dried chili

1 clove garlic, crushed

handful arugula (rocket) or young spinach leaves

Tagliatelle with Morel Mushrooms & Cream

METHOD

1 *Prepare the mushrooms by splitting lengthwise. Rinse and dry with a paper towel. Set aside about 2 oz (60 g) of the morels for garnishing.*

2 *Melt the butter in a pan and sweat the mushrooms.*

3 *Add the shallots and sauté for a few minutes. Add the wine and cook to reduce by two-thirds.*

4 *Meanwhile, bring a large saucepan of salted water to a boil, then add the tagliatelle. Once the water has returned to a boil, lower the heat and simmer with the lid off until the pasta is cooked al dente.*

5 *When the pasta is almost cooked, pour the cream into the pan containing the mushrooms and bring to a boil, then reduce heat to just keep warm.*

6 *Drain the pasta and return to the saucepan. Pour in the cream sauce and stir through.*

To serve: *Spoon a generous serving of pasta onto each of 4 large plates and decorate with the remaining morel mushrooms.*

Ingredients

serves 4

14 oz (440 g) morel mushrooms

4 tbsp (2 oz/60 g) butter

$1/2$ cup (2 oz/60 g) chopped shallots

scant 1 cup (7 fl oz/220 ml) dry white wine

salt

1 lb (500 g) fresh tagliatelle

$1^{1}/_{3}$ cups (11 fl oz/330 ml) heavy (double) cream

Terrine of Porcini & Herbs

Ingredients

serves 4

1 clove garlic, finely chopped

1 bunch fresh parsley, finely chopped

1 bunch fresh dill, chopped

7 oz (220 g) porcini (cèpe) mushrooms, sliced

$^1/_2$ cup (4 fl oz/125 ml) cream

3 eggs, lightly beaten

salt & pepper

2 tbsp butter

2 oz (60 g) chanterelle (girolle) mushrooms

1 bunch fresh chives, chopped

METHOD

1 *Mix together the garlic, herbs, and half of the porcini in a bowl, reserving 4 parsley sprigs for garnish.*

2 *When mixed through, add the cream and eggs. Mix well to achieve a smooth paste and season with salt and pepper to taste.*

3 *Heat half the butter in a frying pan and sauté the rest of the porcini. Remove from the pan and combine with the other mixture.*

4 *Pour the mushroom mixture into a 6-cup terrine. Bake in a 375°F (190°C) oven for 50 minutes. Remove from the oven and allow to cool for 5 hours before serving.*

5 *Just prior to serving, clean the chanterelle mushrooms and lightly sauté in a frying pan with the remaining 1 tablespoon butter. Remove from the pan and drain.*

To serve: *Thickly slice the terrine and place a slice on each plate. Garnish each with a sprig of parsley, and arrange the chanterelles and chives around the edge of the plate.*

Cannellini & Porcini Soup

METHOD

1 *Heat half of the vegetable oil in a pan, add the onion, leek, celery, and 2 cloves of the chopped garlic and sweat until soft.*
2 *Add the cannellini beans, thyme, bay leaf, and rosemary, reserving a sprig for garnish. Add the wine and cook until the liquid reduces. Add the stock, bring to a boil, reduce to a simmer, and cook for 2–2 ¹/₂ hours, or until the beans are tender.*
3 *When the soup is almost cooked, season with salt and pepper. Heat the remaining 1 tablespoon oil in a pan and sauté the porcini with the remaining clove of garlic for a couple of minutes, then add to the beans. Cook for a few more minutes before serving.*

To serve: *Ladle a generous portion into each soup bowl and garnish with a twist of pepper. Strip the leaves from the remaining rosemary sprig and sprinkle over the top.*

Ingredients

serves 4

2 tbsp good-quality vegetable oil

1 onion, finely chopped

1 leek, finely diced

¹/₂ head celery, finely diced

3 cloves garlic, chopped

1 cup (7 oz/220 g) dried cannellini beans, soaked overnight

1 fresh thyme sprig

1 bay leaf

3 fresh rosemary sprigs

4 tbsp (2 fl oz/60 ml) white wine

2 qt (2 l) vegetable stock

salt & pepper

6–7 oz (185–220 g) porcini, (cèpe) mushrooms, diced

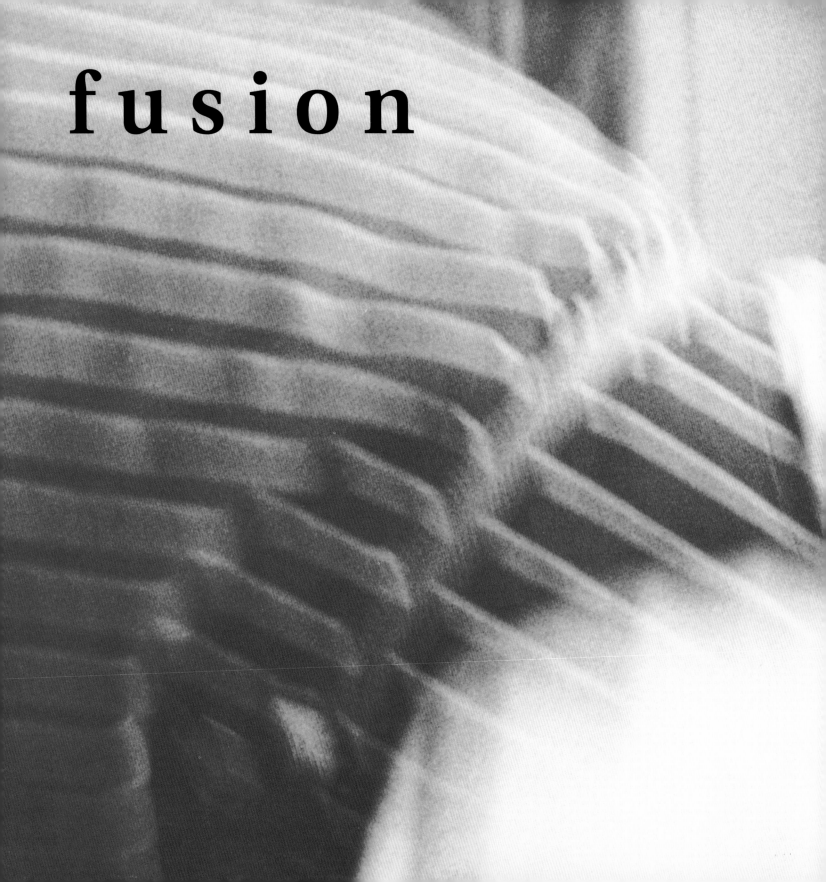

fusion

- Grilled Fillet of John Dory, Celeriac Juice & Mousseron Mushrooms

- Lamb Saddle with Trompettes de la Mort

- Morels & Young Green Vegetables in a Rosemary Bouillon

- Charcoal-Grilled Veal Cutlet with Sweet Potato, Wild Mushrooms & Beurre Noisette

- Panfried Mushrooms with Amontillado

- Marinated Lamb Steak with Porcini, Eggplant & Chickpea Stew

- Wild Mushroom Tamales with Basil Sour Cream

- Raw Mushroom Salad with Beet Dressing

- Sea Bass with Sweet & Sour Mushroom Broth

- Trompette, Jerusalem Artichoke, Potato & Pomegranate Salad

- Roast Sea Bass with Chanterelles, Grilled Fennel & Slow-Roast Tomato

- Paris Mushrooms with Egg Strips & Soy Sauce

- Scrambled Eggs with Oyster Mushrooms & Manchego

- Sautéed Belgian Endives with Monkey Head & Shiitake Mushrooms

- Rosemary & Sesame Flatbread with Sauté of Wild Mushrooms,
  Arugula Leaves & Lemon

- Chanterelles, Potato, Cilantro & Egg Brik

- Panfried Mushrooms with Cilantro, Cumin & Lemon

- Huitlacoche Ice Cream in a Sweet Crispy Rice Cup

Ingredients

serves 4

$^1/_2$ celeriac, peeled

4 John Dory or porgy fillets, skinned

salt & pepper

2 tbsp olive oil

2 tbsp heavy (double) cream

knob of unsalted butter

10 oz (315 g) mousseron mushrooms

4 oz (125 g) mizuna leaves, trimmed

$^1/_2$ bunch fresh chives, finely chopped

Grilled Fillet of John Dory with Celeriac Juice & Mousseron Mushrooms

METHOD

1 *Juice the peeled celeriac in an electric juicer and reserve.*

2 *Season the fish fillets on both sides with salt and pepper. Brush lightly with olive oil. Grill both sides of the fillets over a hot charcoal fire or on a stove-top grill pan. Remove and set aside on a baking sheet (tray).*

3 *Place the celeriac juice in a saucepan and bring to a boil. Add the cream and butter, and whisk with an immersion-blender or a whisk.*

4 *Place a tablespoon of olive oil in a very hot pan, then add the mousseron mushrooms. Sauté for approximately 2 minutes and season with salt and pepper. Remove from the pan and drain on paper towels. Wilt the mizuna leaves in the same pan over low heat for 1 minute, then remove and drain on paper towels.*

5 *Place the fish fillets under a hot broiler (griller) for 4–5 minutes.*

6 *While the fish is cooking, combine the celeriac juice, chives, salt, and pepper in a blender and blend well.*

To serve: *Place a pile of the mizuna leaves in the center of each serving plate, and place a fish fillet on top. Scatter the sautéed mushrooms around. Spoon the celeriac juice around the plate and serve.*

Lamb Saddle with Trompettes de la Mort

METHOD

1 Grind the dried mushrooms to a medium-fine powder in a spice mill.

2 Season the lamb with salt and pepper. Coat with flour and egg, then coat well with the mushroom powder.

3 Chop the lamb bones and place on a baking sheet (tray) with the mirepoix. Bake in a 400°F (200°C) oven for 30 minutes. Remove to a saucepan, add the water and simmer for 30 minutes. Strain, then return to the pan simmer for 20 minutes, or until reduced by a quarter. Reserve. Reheat gravy before serving.

4 Sear the lamb in a hot pan, about 20 seconds on each side, then transfer to the oven and cook at 325°F (165°C) for 7–8 minutes (medium-rare) or 9–12 minutes (medium).

5 Mix the taro, potato, and oil, season, and fry on both sides in a small pan to form 4 cakes. Remove, drain, and reserve.

6 Purée the green onions in a blender. Remove to a pan and heat gently. Add 1½ tablespoons of the butter, salt, and pepper.

7 Melt the remaining butter in a pan and add the lemongrass, shallots and chili. Sweat for a few minutes, then add the oyster mushrooms and sauté. Season with a little salt.

To serve: *Slice the lamb into thirds and arrange with purée around the mushrooms. Finish with a drizzle of gravy and serve with potato cakes.*

Ingredients

serves 4

14 oz (440 g) dried trompette de la mort mushrooms

2 lamb loins, fat removed & cut in half (from 1 short saddle), bones reserved

salt & pepper

1 cup all-purpose (plain) flour

3 eggs, lightly beaten

about 1½ cups (6 oz/185 g) diced vegetable mirepoix (carrot, leek, onion, celery)

2 cups (16 fl oz/500 ml) water

8 oz (250 g) taro, matchstick sliced on mandoline

8 oz (250 g) potato, matchstick sliced on mandoline

4 tbsp (2 fl oz/60 ml) vegetable oil

12 green (spring) onions, green parts sliced & blanched

2 tbsp unsalted butter

1 lemongrass stalk, trimmed & finely chopped

4 shallots, finely chopped

½ chili, very finely chopped

10 oz (315 g) oyster mushrooms

Morels & Young Green Vegetables in a Rosemary Bouillon

Ingredients

serves 4

1 cup (4 oz/125 g) shelled fava (broad) beans

³/₄ cup (4 oz/125 g) shelled peas

4 oz (125 g) asparagus spears, trimmed

4 oz (125 g) snow peas (mangetouts)

4 oz (125 g) sugar snap peas

4 oz (125 g) arugula (rocket) leaves

4 oz (125 g) baby spinach leaves

4 tbsp (2 oz/60 g) butter

10 oz (315 g) morel mushrooms

1 cup (8 fl oz/250 ml) chicken stock or vegetable stock

1 fresh rosemary sprig

¹/₂ cup (4 fl oz/125 ml) double (heavy) cream

salt & white pepper

METHOD

1 *Blanch all the green vegetables separately in boiling, salted water and refresh in ice water. Peel the favas. Put aside on paper towels to drain.*

2 *Place half of the butter in a heavy saucepan and heat until it starts to bubble.*

3 *Add the morels and cook until they start to become soft, then add the stock and rosemary sprig, and cook to reduce by half.*

4 *Add the cream to the morel bouillon, return to a boil, then add the remaining butter and mix in.*

5 *Add the blanched vegetables to the bouillon, except the arugula and spinach. Bring to a boil and season.*

6 *Add the arugula and baby spinach leaves at the last minute. Remove from the heat and serve immediately.*

To serve: *Arrange the vegetables in a pile in the center of a soup plate and spoon the bouillon around.*

Charcoal-Grilled Veal Cutlet with Sweet Potato, Wild Mushrooms & Beurre Noisette

METHOD

1 *Cook the sweet potatoes in boiling salted water until tender. Drain. Meanwhile clean the wild mushrooms.*

2 *Prepare a charcoal fire or preheat a ridged stove-top grill pan. Season the veal cutlets and coat with 1 tablespoon of the olive oil. Sear on both sides over charcoal or on the grill pan, then cook until done as desired. Remove and keep warm.*

3 *Diagonally slice the sweet potatoes lengthwise into 3 strips. Grill over hot coals or on grill pan.*

4 *Heat half of the butter and 1 tablespoon of olive oil in a pan and sauté the wild mushrooms. Remove and drain.*

5 *Heat the remainder of the butter in the pan until it turns nut brown. Add the veal stock, capers, lemon juice, and seasoning and heat through. Meanwhile, dress the arugula with the remaining 2 tablespoons of olive oil and the balsamic vinegar.*

To serve: *Place a veal cutlet in the middle of each plate and spoon the wild mushrooms over them. Place a slice of sweet potato to one side and spoon over the butter mixture. Garnish each plate with a lemon wedge and some of the arugula salad.*

Ingredients

serves 4

2 sweet potatoes

salt & pepper

10 oz (315 g) mixed wild mushrooms

4 tbsp (2 fl oz/60 ml) extra-virgin olive oil

veal cutlets (best end), 8 oz (250 g) each

2 tbsp butter

4 tbsp (2 fl oz/60 ml) veal stock

4 tbsp (1 oz/30 g) small capers

juice of $1/2$ lemon

4 oz (125 g) arugula (rocket)

1 tbsp balsamic vinegar

1 lemon, cut into quarters

Panfried Mushrooms with Amontillado

Ingredients

serves 4

enough olive oil to cover the bottom of your frying pan

1 small onion, finely chopped

1 clove garlic, finely chopped

1 lb (500 g) mixed wild mushrooms such as chanterelle (girolle), porcini (cèpe), and trompette de la mort, sliced

$^1/_2$ cup (4 fl oz/125 ml) dry or aged Amontillado or fino sherry

pinch ground nutmeg

salt & pepper

3 tbsp chopped fresh flat-leaf parsley

4 slices toast, 1 clove garlic, & 1 tbsp olive oil to serve

METHOD

1 *Heat the olive oil in a large frying pan over medium heat, add the onion, and cook until translucent.*

2 *Add the garlic and cook for a further 5 minutes, stirring well so that the garlic and onion do not burn.*

3 *Turn up the heat, add the mushrooms, and cook for 1 minute. Add the Amontillado or fino sherry and nutmeg.*

4 *Cook for a further minute, meanwhile stirring in the salt, pepper, and the chopped parsley.*

To serve: *Heap mounds of the mushrooms on slices of toast rubbed with a little garlic and drizzled with olive oil*

Marinated Lamb Steak with Porcini, Eggplant & Chickpea Stew

Ingredients

serves 4

4 lamb steaks

6 tbsp (3 fl oz/90 ml) olive oil

zest of 1 lemon

few fresh thyme sprigs

2 cloves garlic, crushed

4 Asian (slender) eggplants (aubergines)

2 red onions, chopped

6–7 oz (185–220 g) porcini (cèpe) mushrooms

1 tsp ground cumin

1 tsp ground coriander

large pinch paprika

1 tbsp tomato paste

4 tomatoes, chopped

1 can (8 oz/250 g) chick peas (garbanzo beans), drained

2 tbsp chopped fresh cilantro (coriander)

METHOD

1 *Marinate the lamb steaks in 4 tablespoons (2 fl oz/60 ml) of the olive oil, the lemon zest, thyme, and 1 garlic clove for at least 24 hours.*

2 *Cut the eggplants into small cubes. Fry in the remaining 2 tablespoons olive oil over medium heat with the red onion and the remaining garlic, until soft.*

3 *Cut the mushrooms into quarters and add to the pan, frying for a further 2 minutes.*

4 *Add the cumin, coriander, paprika, and tomato paste.*

5 *Add the tomatoes and bring to a boil. Then simmer for 45 minutes, stirring occasionally.*

6 *About 5 minutes before the stew is ready, add the chick-peas to the tomato and mushroom stew.*

7 *Place the lamb steaks in a hot frying pan and use some of the marinade oil to fry them. Color each side for 2 minutes.*

8 *Add most of the chopped cilantro and stir, then remove from the heat and serve.*

To serve: *Arrange a lamb steak and helping of stew on each plate. Finish with the remaining cilantro and drizzle with a little olive oil.*

Wild Mushroom Tamales with Basil Sour Cream

METHOD

1 *Soak the dried porcini in the warm water for an hour, then drain and chop finely.*

2 *Heat the olive oil in a large, heavy pan and sauté the porcini and wild mushrooms. Season with salt and pepper and remove from the pan.*

3 *Melt the butter in the pan and sweat the onion, garlic, and chili until soft. Add the cooked mushrooms and white wine. Simmer to reduce the wine, then add the stock. Bring to a boil and add the quinoa. Simmer until tender.*

4 *Add the polenta and cook for a further few minutes. It should be the consistency of risotto; if not, then add more stock as necessary. Let cool.*

5 *Mold a big ball of the mixture and press in the center of a corn husk, roll up between the palms into a sausage shape, and twist each end. Tie each end with a strip of husk. Repeat with remaining husks.*

6 *Place the tamales on a baking sheet (tray) and bake in a 375°F (190°C) oven for 20 minutes.*

7 *Meanwhile, purée the basil with the sour cream and 1 clove garlic. When the tamales are cooked, let cool slightly.*

To serve: *Make a small lengthwise slit down the middle of each tamale, then push ends together to open out as you would a baked potato. Top with basil dressing and serve with arugula and tomato salad.*

Ingredients

serves 4

1 oz (30 g) dried porcini (cèpe) mushrooms

$^1/_2$ cup (4 fl oz/125 ml) water

4 tbsp (2 fl oz/60 ml) olive oil

1 lb (500 g) mixed wild mushrooms

salt & pepper

4 tbsp (2 oz/60 g) butter

1 white onion, finely chopped

3 cloves garlic, chopped

1 large red chili, sliced

$^3/_4$ cup (6 fl oz/180 ml) white wine

4 cups (32 fl oz/1 l) chicken stock

8 oz (250 g) quinoa

$^1/_3$ cup (2 oz/60 g) polenta

dried corn husks, soaked in water for 6 hours & drained

leaves from 1 bunch fresh basil

scant 1 cup (7 fl oz/220 ml) sour cream

1 clove garlic

arugula (rocket) and tomato salad to serve

Raw Mushroom Salad with Beet Dressing

METHOD

1 *First prepare the dressing. Place the chopped beets in a blender with 2 tablespoons of the olive oil, the balsamic vinegar, salt, pepper, and water, and process until smooth. Pass through a fine sieve and set aside until ready to serve.*
2 *Slice the mushrooms, place in a bowl, and season. Add the lemon juice and the remaining 2 tablespoons olive oil, mix well, and leave for 10 minutes, mixing every 2 minutes.*
3 *Add the arugula and chives to the mushrooms and mix gently through.*

To serve: *Arrange a base of overlapping beet slices in the center of each plate and place a mound of the mushrooms on top. Spoon the beet dressing and the juice from the mushrooms around the mound.*

Ingredients

serves 4

3 oz (90 g) cooked beets (beetroot), finely chopped

4 tbsp (2 fl oz/60 ml) olive oil

2 tbsp balsamic vinegar

salt & pepper

3 tbsp water

10 oz (315 g) firm white mushrooms

juice of $1/2$ lemon

2 handfuls arugula (rocket) leaves

2 tbsp finely chopped, fresh chives

6–7 oz (185–220 g) cooked beets (beetroot), thinly sliced

Ingredients

serves 4

4 hazelnuts (filberts)

4 almonds

1 tbsp coriander seeds

1 tbsp sesame seeds

$^1/_2$ tbsp pepper

$^2/_3$ cup (5 oz/155 g) butter

2 lb (1 kg) button
mushrooms, sliced

5 tbsp (4 oz/125 g) honey

1 tbsp lime juice

5 tbsp (2$^1/_2$ fl oz/75 ml) sherry
vinegar

5 tbsp (2$^1/_2$ fl oz/75 ml) soy
sauce

4 cups (32 fl oz/1 l) spring
water

sea bass fillets, 4–5 oz
(125-155 g) each

salt & pepper

5 tbsp heavy (double) cream

$^1/_2$ cup (3 oz/90 g) diced and
blanched butternut squash

2 oz (60 g) trompette de la
mort mushrooms

2 oz (60 g) honshimeji
mushrooms

4 pearl onions, halved &
blanched

1 slice bacon, chopped and fried

4 oz (125 g) spinach, chopped

$^1/_2$ tsp chopped chili

lime juice to taste

Sea Bass with Sweet & Sour Mushroom Broth

METHOD

1 *Toast the nuts and seeds on a baking sheet (tray) under a broiler (griller). Remove, add pepper, and grind in a spice mill, or by hand.*

2 *The broth can be made in advance and then reheated just prior to serving. Melt some of the butter in a frying pan and sauté the mushrooms in small batches until golden, adding more butter if necessary (but reserve a knob for later). When all the mushrooms are cooked, return them to the pan, add the honey, and cook until caramelized. Deglaze with the tablespoon of lime juice.*

3 *Add the vinegar, soy sauce, and water, bring to a boil, and simmer for 30 minutes. Strain and reserve.*

4 *About 10 minutes before you are ready to serve, reheat broth. Meanwhile, season the bass, dip one side into cream, and then into the ground mixed spice. Sauté in a frying pan over medium heat until golden. Remove from the pan.*

5 *Melt the remaining butter and sauté the squash, mushrooms and onion. Add bacon and spinach, stir, and remove from heat. Season the broth with chili, lime juice, and salt.*

To serve: *Arrange a portion of vegetables on each plate, pour over the broth, and place a sea bass fillet on top.*

Trompette, Jerusalem Artichoke, Potato & Pomegranate Salad

METHOD

1 *Clean the mushrooms, and marinate with the garlic, half of the pomegranate juice, half of the olive oil, and half of the mint. Marinate for at least 30 minutes.*

2 *Boil the Jerusalem artichokes and potatoes in salted water. Refresh in cold water, cut into quarters, and place in a large bowl. Add the onion and the rest of the mint, chopped, as well as some pomegranate seeds.*

3 *Add the mushrooms and arugula leaves. Mix the rest of the pomegranate juice and olive oil with the balsamic vinegar and dress the salad, reserving a little of the dressing.*

To serve: *Arrange the salad on plates, finishing with a further drizzle of dressing and a sprinkling of pomegranate seeds.*

Ingredients

serves 4

10 oz (315 g) trompette de la mort mushrooms

1 clove garlic, crushed

1 pomegranate, juice extracted & some seeds reserved

1 cup (8 fl oz/250 ml) olive oil

2 cups (2 oz/60 g) fresh mint leaves

10 oz (315 g) Jerusalem artichokes

10 oz (315 g) new potatoes

salt

1 red onion, chopped

2 large handfuls arugula (rocket) leaves

4 tbsp (2 fl oz/60 ml) balsamic vinegar

Roast Sea Bass with Chanterelles, Grilled Fennel & Slow-Roast Tomato

Ingredients

serves 4

2 plum (Roma) tomatoes

1–2 tbsp extra-virgin olive oil

4 baby fennel bulbs, trimmed (trimmings reserved)

salt & pepper

6–7 oz (185–200 g) chanterelle (girolle) mushrooms

2 sea bass, 2 lb (1 kg) each gutted, head & tail removed, cut in half crosswise

³/₄ cup (4 oz/125 g) olives

4 tbsp (2 fl oz/60 ml) fish stock

4 tbsp (2 oz/60 g) unsalted butter

1 large lemon, cut into quarters

METHOD

1 *Cut the tomatoes in half and lay on a lightly oiled baking sheet (tray) with the trimmed ends of the fennel. Season with salt and pepper and brush with olive oil. Roast in the oven at 475°F (240°C) for about 20 minutes. Remove and allow to cool. Reduce the oven temperature to 400°F (200°C).*

2 *While the tomatoes roast, blanch the fennel, then rinse in cold water. Cut the fennel bulbs in half lengthwise and remove the center core, then slice lengthwise into thin strips. Clean the mushrooms and set aside.*

3 *Sear the sea bass portions quickly on both sides in a hot ovenproof pan and then place in the oven for 8 minutes, or until done.*

4 *Meanwhile, grill the fennel strips over a charcoal fire. (If using an oven, place the fennel strips on an oiled pan and roast in a 400°F (200°C) oven for 15 minutes, before cooking the sea bass.)*

5 *Place the olives in the fish stock and leave to warm over low heat. Meanwhile, gently fry the mushrooms in butter.*

To serve: *Place the bass on a large plate and garnish with the tomato, olives, mushrooms, grilled fennel, and a lemon quarter. Pour a spoonful of the fish stock over the top. (As an option, drizzle salsa verde over and around the fish.)*

Paris Mushrooms with Egg Strips & Soy Sauce

METHOD

1 *To make the egg strips, whisk 3 eggs with a pinch of salt and pepper, a pinch of sugar, and 1 tablespoon of water. Lightly oil a nonstick frying pan and place over medium heat until hot. Pour in enough egg mixture to coat the pan thinly, tilting to distribute it evenly. Cook until the egg is just dry but not browned on the bottom. Remove to a plate to cool, and repeat until the egg mixture is used up.*

2 *When cool, roll up each omelet and slice into strips 1/4 inch (6 mm) wide.*

3 *Place the garlic and ginger in a small saucepan with the soy sauce, remaining water, a pinch of sugar, and pepper and bring to a boil. Lower heat and simmer until reduced by half, then strain.*

4 *Put the sesame oil in a frying pan big enough to hold the mushrooms and place over high heat. Sauté the mushrooms for a few minutes, then add the soy sauce mixture. Reduce the heat to medium and cook for about 15 minutes, or until the liquid is reduced to a thick syrup.*

5 *Add the egg strips to the mushroom mixture and toss lightly. Remove from the heat and serve immediately.*

To serve: *Place equal portions on 4 plates and garnish with the thinly sliced green onions and toasted sesame seeds.*

Ingredients

serves 4

3 eggs

salt & pepper

2 pinches sugar

2/3 cup (5 fl oz/150 ml) water

1/2 tbsp vegetable oil

1 clove garlic, finely chopped

1-inch (2–5 cm) piece ginger, peeled & finely chopped

2/3 cup (5 fl oz/150 ml) soy sauce

2 tbsp Asian sesame oil

8 oz (250 g) Paris (button) mushrooms

2 green (spring) onions, thinly sliced

small handful toasted sesame seeds

Ingredients

serves 4

8 eggs

scant 1 cup (7 fl oz/220 ml) heavy (double) cream

salt & pepper

3 tbsp olive oil

1 lb (500 g) oyster mushrooms

4 cloves garlic, chopped

handful chopped, fresh, flat-leaf parsley

1³/₄ cups (7 oz/220 g) grated Manchego cheese

4 slices coarse country bread, toasted

Scrambled Eggs with Oyster Mushrooms & Manchego

METHOD

1 *Beat the eggs with the cream and season with salt and pepper.*

2 *Heat 2 tablespoons of the olive oil in a frying pan until it is smoking and fry the mushrooms until browned.*

3 *Stir in the garlic, cook for a minute, then add half the parsley. Season with salt and pepper. Remove the mushrooms from the pan and reserve.*

4 *Heat the remaining tablespoon oil in another pan until just hot. Add the egg-and-cream mixture, stirring constantly until it is the texture of thick cream. Do not overcook.*

5 *Stir in half the mushrooms and half the cheese, and remove from heat.*

To serve: *Place a helping of the eggs on toast, and scatter over the remaining cheese, mushrooms, and parsley.*

Sautéed Belgian Endives with Monkey Head & Shiitake Mushrooms

Ingredients

8 heads baby Belgian endives (chicory/witloof)

salt

4 tbsp (2 oz/60 g) butter

4 tbsp (2 fl oz/60 ml) walnut oil

1 red onion, finely chopped

8 oz (250 g) monkey head mushrooms

8 oz (250 g) shiitake mushrooms

2 oz (60 g) dandelion leaves

2 oz (60 g) arugula (rocket) leaves

juice of 1 lemon

2¼ cups (18 fl oz/625 ml) strong mushroom stock

1 oz (30 g) dried porcini (cèpe) mushrooms

2¼ cups (18 fl oz/625 ml) heavy (double) cream

METHOD

1 *Blanch the endives whole in salted water and refresh. Split in half lengthwise. Heat the butter and walnut oil in a pan and sauté the endives. Remove from the pan.*

2 *In the still-moist pan, sauté the red onion and the monkey head, and shiitake mushrooms. Remove from the heat and set to one side. Meanwhile, mix the dandelion and arugula leaves, and dress with the lemon juice.*

3 *Make the sauce just prior to serving. Bring the mushroom stock to a boil. Reduce the heat and simmer until reduced by half. Add the dried porcini and cream and bring to a boil. Remove from the heat.*

To serve: *Arrange 4 pieces of endive in each bowl. Add the onion-mushroom mixture to the arugula mixture and arrange neatly on plate. Pour the warm sauce over and around the salad.*

Rosemary & Sesame Flatbread with Sauté of Wild Mushrooms, Arugula Leaves & Lemon

METHOD

1 *Make the flatbread in advance. Combine the yeast and 2¹/₄ cups (11 oz/330 g) flour in a bowl. Stir in the water. Cover and let stand in a warm place for 25 minutes, or until frothy.*

2 *Place the 3 cups (1 lb/450 g) flour and the salt in a large bowl. Add the yeast mixture and half the oil and mix to a dough. Knead until dough is smooth and elastic. Place in an oiled bowl and let rise until doubled in size.*

3 *Break the dough into 8 pieces and roll each into a thin round. Place on baking sheet (tray), cover, and let rise for a 15 minutes. Roll again, and sprinkle with olive oil, rosemary, and sesame seeds. Bake in a 400°F (200°C) oven for 10 minutes, or until golden brown. Keep warm.*

4 *Heat the butter and half the olive oil in a large frying pan and sauté the wild mushrooms. Remove and drain. Dress the arugula leaves in the remaining olive oil and season.*

To serve: *Place a flatbread on each plate or serve from a basket. Spoon the mushrooms to one side of the bread. Garnish with a lemon wedge and the arugula.*

Ingredients

serves 4

4 tbsp (2 oz/60 g) unsalted butter

¹/₂ cup (4 fl oz/125 ml) extra-virgin olive oil

10 oz (315 g) mixed wild mushrooms

4 oz (125 g) arugula (rocket) leaves

salt & pepper

1 large lemon, cut into quarters

for the flatbread

1 tsp active dry yeast

2¹/₄ cups (11 oz/330 ml) all-purpose (plain) flour, plus 3 cups (1 lb/450 g)

2 cups (16 fl oz/500 ml) water

large pinch salt

6 tbsp (3 fl oz/90 ml) olive oil

2 tbsp sesame seeds

2 tbsp chopped, fresh rosemary

Chanterelle, Potato, Cilantro & Egg Brik

Ingredients

serves 4

3 medium potatoes

knob of butter

2 tbsp milk

10 oz (315 g) chanterelle (girolle) mushrooms

1 tbsp vegetable oil

1 red chili, seeded & chopped

2 cloves garlic, crushed

1 red onion, chopped

³/₄ cup (4 oz/125 g) pitted black olives, chopped

¹/₂ bunch fresh cilantro (coriander), chopped

salt & pepper

8 spring roll wrappers

4 raw egg yolks

vegetable oil for deep-frying

handful salad greens

METHOD

1 *Boil the potatoes until soft, then mash with a little butter and milk.*

2 *Clean the mushrooms. Heat the oil in a hot frying pan and fry the mushrooms, along with the chili and garlic, until soft.*

3 *Mix the chopped onion, chopped black olives, and cilantro into the potato and season with salt and pepper.*

4 *Place a little of the potato mix in the center of each of 4 spring roll wrappers, making a well in the center of the mix.*

5 *Place an egg yolk into each well, then scatter the mushrooms on the top. Fold the edges of the pastry gently over the mix to create a square. Then take another sheet of pastry and fold around to create a secure parcel.*

6 *Deep-fry in 350°F (180°C) oil for 2–3 minutes, or until golden, then drain and serve.*

To serve: *Slice each parcel in half and arrange on plate with a scattering of salad greens.*

Panfried Mushrooms with Cilantro, Cumin & Lemon

METHOD

1 *Before you start cooking, have all the ingredients sliced or chopped.*

2 *Heat the olive oil in a large frying pan over medium to high heat and add the garlic.*

3 *As soon as the garlic starts to color, add the mushrooms and ground cumin.*

4 *Stir for a minute or so, then add the cilantro, salt, pepper, and lemon juice. Leave over the heat for another few seconds, then remove.*

To serve: *Serve with warm flatbread, a dollop of spiced, seasoned yogurt, and salad on the side.*

Ingredients

enough olive oil just to cover the bottom of the frying pan

2 cloves garlic, roughly chopped

500g (1 lb/2 oz) mixed wild mushrooms such as chanterelle, porcini, trompette de la mort, sliced

$\frac{1}{2}$ tsp ground cumin

3 tbsp roughly chopped fresh cilantro (coriander)

salt & pepper

juice of 1 lemon

4 rounds flatbread

4 tbsp (2 oz/60 g) yogurt, seasoned with salt, pepper, crushed cumin seeds & crushed garlic

handful mixed salad greens

Huitlacoche Ice Cream in a Sweet Crispy Rice Cup

Ingredients

serves 4

for the rice cup

²/₃ cup (4 oz/125 g) Thai sticky (glutinous) rice

4 cups (32 fl oz/1 l) water

scant 1 cup (6¹/₂ oz/200 g) superfine (caster) sugar

oil for deep-frying

for the topping

²/₃ cup (3¹/₂ oz/100 g) frozen corn kernels, thawed

3 tbsp superfine (caster) sugar

for the ice cream

²/₃ cup (4 oz/100 g) superfine (caster) sugar

6 egg yolks

1 cup (8 fl oz/250 ml) milk

1 cup (8 fl oz/250 ml) heavy (double) cream

¹/₂ vanilla bean (pod), split

4 oz (125 g) frozen huitlacoche (black corn fungus), thawed

METHOD

1 *Mix the rice and water in a saucepan and cook over low heat until the rice is tender. Dissolve the sugar in the mixture, remove from the heat, let cool for 5 minutes, and pour it onto a baking sheet (tray) lined with parchment. To make the topping: spread the corn on a baking sheet and sprinkle with the sugar. Place both the rice and corn in a preheated 175°F (80°C) oven overnight, until they are dry, hard, and crispy.*

2 *Fill a large, heavy pan ¹/₃ full of oil and heat to 400°F (200°C) on a deep-frying thermometer. Snap the dry rice sheet into 4 squares and using tongs, place each in the hot oil. As the rice puffs and turns golden, transfer each square onto an upturned bowl. Immediately place another bowl on top. When cool, remove the bowls.*

3 *In a bowl, whisk together the sugar and yolks. Boil the milk, cream, and vanilla in a saucepan; remove from the heat and discard the bean. Add ¹/₄ of the hot milk to the yolks, whisking all the time. Add the yolk mixture to the hot milk still in the pan. Return to the heat, and cook, stirring until thickened. Remove from the heat and whisk in the huitlacoche, then pour through a sieve into a bowl. Cool by placing the bowl over ice water. Freeze in an ice cream maker according to the manufacturer's instructions.*

To serve: *Center each rice cup on a plate, and place a few corn kernels in each cup. Scoop the ice cream into the cups, and garnish with the rest of the corn. Serve immediately.*

glossary

Amontillado

Aged, amber-colored dry sherry.

Asafoetida

A root extract from India that adds pungency to Asian dishes.

Black Beans

Flavorful salted Chinese beans, available whole in cans or jars, or dried. Use sparingly, as they tend to be very salty.

Cannellini Beans

A white bean with a nutty taste, available fresh in the summer or canned year-round. Dried cannellini beans should be soaked overnight before use. The bean originates from Argentina and is used widely in Italy for soups and stews.

Celeriac

A root vegetable similar in taste to celery. Once the thick skin has been peeled, it can be used julienned raw in salads, or in dressings, soups and sauces.

Chaat Masala

An Indian spice powder of cloves, cumin, chili, mint, rock salt, ginger, and dried mango.

Cha-Soba

Japanese buckwheat noodles made with green tea, giving them a bright green appearance.

Curry Leaves

Aromatic leaves that can be bought fresh or dried from large Asian grocery stores.

Daikon

A long white radish used in Japanese, Korean, and Chinese cooking. Usually served raw, thinly sliced, or shredded.

Duxelle

A dry, cooked mushroom mix used to intensify the flavor of soups and stews.

A basic duxelle recipe:
Ingredients
1 tsp butter
$1/2$ onion, finely chopped
1 lb (500 g) mushrooms of choice, finely chopped
salt & pepper

Method
Melt the butter in a frying pan and sauté the onion until soft. Add the mushrooms, season and then cook over high heat, stirring until the liquid has evaporated and you are left with a dry, concentrated mixture.

Foie Gras

The fattened liver of a duck or goose can be bought raw from specialty butchers. It comes in the form of two lobes, which should be slit and trimmed of all veins and any remaining gall bladder. If prepared in a terrine, raw foie gras needs slow cooking at low heat. Fresh foie gras can also be sliced and sautéed in butter, to be served with fruits or in salads.

Galanga

A variety of ginger, with a very pungent flavor, used widely in Southeast Asian cooking.

Honshimeji

A Japanese mushroom with a small, rounded head and gray-white flesh.

Huitlacoche

A sweet-tasting fungus that grows on corn. Also known as black corn fungus or mushroom.

Jerusalem Artichoke

This pale root vegetable can be used in much the same way as a potato, deep-fried, boiled, or baked. It is usually blanched before cooking to prevent discoloring.

Konbu

Sea kelp, used dry as a key ingredient in many Japanese stocks and soups.

Lemongrass

A fragrant grass used in Southeast Asian cooking. The stalk should be peeled and only the pale section at the base used. It is usually cut into segments and added to soups and stews, and may be removed from the dish before serving. When not available fresh, substitute frozen.

Lotus Root

A water lily root used in Japanese and Chinese cooking.

Manchego

A popular Spanish sheep's cheese from La Mancha, Manchego is a hard cheese with a full flavor.

Masa harina

Dried corn that is ground and treated to form the basis of masa, or tamale dough.

Mirin

A sweet Japanese rice wine used in cooking, particularly for sauces and marinades.

Monkey Head Mushrooms

A round, white Asian mushroom about the size of a tennis ball, covered in a coat of fine, hairlike fibers, hence the name.

Mushroom Stock

A flavorful stock of mushroom can be made by simmering an assortment of mushrooms in stock water. In addition to mushroom, one can add onion, leek, garlic, ginger, soysauce, or bouquet garni. Generally, 5 cups of vegetables in 6 cups of water will yield 3 to 4 cups of stock. Substitute water, or store-bought vegetable stock.

Nori

Crisp, flat sheets of Japanese seaweed used to wrap sushi. They can also be shredded for use as a garnish.

Okra

Green, pod-shaped vegetable with a gelatinous flesh that helps to thicken stews and gumbos.

Pickled Ginger

Fine, pale pink slices of ginger that have been pickled for a light sweet-and-sour taste. It is typically served as an accompaniment to sashimi and sushi.

Ponzu

A Japanese dressing containing musk lime, vinegar, and soy sauce. Also used as a marinade.

Quinoa

A highly nutritious ricelike grain, native to South America.

Ragout

A traditional stew of meat and vegetables, but the word is often used to refer to any stewed dish.

Ramen

Thick, Chinese-style egg noodles used extensively in Japanese soups and stir-fries.

Samphire

A coastal plant traditionally used as an accompaniment to seafood dishes in Britain and France. It can be eaten boiled or steamed, blanched or pickled.

Shiso

Otherwise known as beefsteak plant, the leaf of the shiso has a peppery taste and is typically used raw as a garnish.

Star Anise

A staple Asian spice in the form of a star-shaped seed with a flavor akin to that of aniseed. Ideal in fish and seafood dishes.

Taro

A root vegetable grown in Asia and the Caribbean.

Truffles

The two most common varieties of this rare fungus are the black truffle from Périgord in France and the white Alba truffle from Italy. In season from mid-November to March, the fresh black truffle has a crumbly texture and a delicate flavor similar to that of vanilla. By contrast, the white truffle has a smooth beige skin and hard, brittle flesh. It is best appreciated when freshly grated over dishes such as pasta and risotto.

Wasabi

A Japanese horseradish paste that always accompanies sushi.

contributors

Christian Delteil
BANK

◆ *Carpaccio of Beef, Bruschetta & Wild Mushrooms (p. 82)*
◆ *Crostini with Chanterelles, Poached Egg & Pesto Dressing (p. 92)*
◆ *Tagliatelle with Morel Mushrooms & Cream (p. 108)*

Henry Brereton
CANTALOUPE

◆ *Charcoal-Grilled Veal Cutlet with Sweet Potato, Wild Mushrooms & Beurre Noisette (p. 122)*
◆ *Roast Sea Bass with Chanterelle, Grilled Fennel & Slow-Roast Tomato (p. 136)*
◆ *Rosemary & Sesame Flatbread with Sauté of Wild Mushrooms, Arugula Leaves & Lemon (p. 144)*

Cyrus Todiwala
CAFE SPICE NAMASTE

◆ *Oyster Mushroom Sukha Masala (p. 16)*
◆ *Enoki Mushrooms with Ginger, Garlic & Chili (p. 26)*
◆ *Mushrooms Manchurian (p. 32)*
◆ *Mushrooms in Hot Garlic Sauce (p. 42)*

Adrian Searing
CHRISTOPHER'S

◆ *Grilled Mushrooms on Texas Toast with Texas Steak Sauce (p. 62)*
◆ *Wild Morel Tamale with Pico de Gallo & Cilantro Oil (p. 66)*
◆ *Roast Lamb with Wild Mushroom Hash Browns (p. 75)*

Adam Gray
COAST

◆ Roasted Porcini Feuillentine (p. 94)

◆ Grilled Fillet of John Dory with Celeriac Juice & Mousseron Mushrooms (p. 116)

◆ Morels & Young Green Vegetables in a Rosemary Bouillon (p. 120)

Chris Benians
DAPHNES

◆ Monkfish, Clams, Samphire & Trompettes de la Mort (p. 68)

◆ Squab, Wild Mushroom & Barolo Risotto (p. 70)

◆ Cannellini & Porcini Soup (p. 112)

Stepehen Wheeler,
Giuseppe Silvestre
THE GEORGIAN, HARRODS

◆ Roast Cod with a Casserole of Shrimp, White Beans & Mushroom Sauce (p. 78)

◆ Herb Tagliatelle with Baby Clams, Garlic & Porcini Mushrooms (p. 90)

◆ Roast Rabbit Leg with Olives, Thyme & Portobello Mushrooms (p. 96)

Cass Titcombe
COLLECTION

◆ Oyster Mushroom & Shiitake Roll (p. 50)

◆ Seared Tuna Sashimi with Shiitake Salad (p. 58)

◆ Wild Mushroom Tamales with Basil Sour Cream (p. 128)

Heston Blumenthal
FAT DUCK

◆ Pork Sausage with Purée of Caramelized Cauliflower (p. 72)

◆ Crepinette of Scallops, Spinach & Porcini with Velouté of Fava Beans & Morels (p. 80)

◆ Lasagna of Shrimp, Pig's Feet & Truffles (p. 84)

Patrick Williams
GREEN'S

◆ Millefeuille of Salmon, Leek & Seasonal Wild Mushrooms (p. 86)

◆ Wild Mushrooms on Thyme Rösti with Leek Sprouts & Sour Cream (p. 88)

◆ Ragout of Mushrooms, Warm Poached Eggs & Black Truffles (p. 102)

◆ Sautéed Belgian Endives with Monkey Head & Shiitake Mushrooms (p. 142)

Thierry Laborde

THE ICON

- *Saucisson de Foie Gras & Champignons Sauvages (p. 98)*
- *Risotto of Foie Gras & Truffles (p. 100)*
- *Terrine of Porcini & Herbs (p. 110)*

Samantha Clark

MORO

- *Panfried Mushrooms with Amontillado (p. 124)*
- *Scrambled Eggs with Oyster Mushrooms & Manchego (p. 140)*
- *Panfried Mushrooms with Cilantro Cumin & Lemon (p. 148)*

Craig Grey

MASH

- *Mushroom Ragout Surprise (p. 64)*
- *Raw Mushroom Salad with Beet Dressing (p. 130)*

James McMurrough,
Jason Sant

PASHA

- *Marinated Lamb Steak with Porcini, Eggplant & Chickpea Stew (p. 126)*
- *Trompette, Jerusalem Artichoke, Potato & Pomegranate Salad (p. 134)*
- *Chanterelle, Potato, Cilantro & Egg Brik (p. 146)*

Mark Gregory

T'SU

◆ *Vegetarian Maki-Zushi with Shiitake & Enoki Mushrooms, Pickles & Avocado (p. 20)*

◆ *Grilled Lemongrass & Ginger Chicken with Cha-Soba (p. 34)*

◆ *Poached Tataki of Tuna with Caramelized Green Onions, Mushroom Salad & Ponzu (p. 40)*

Daniel Del Vecchio,

Shaun Gilmore

VONG

◆ *Asparagus, Enoki & Chili Salad (p. 18)*

◆ *Lamb Saddle with Trompettes de la Mort (p. 118)*

◆ *Sea Bass with Sweet & Sour Mushroom Broth (p. 132)*

◆ *Huitlacoche Ice Cream in a Sweet Crispy Rice Cup (p. 150)*

Ngoc Mai Henry

WOK WOK

◆ *Mushroom & Ginger Stir-fry (p. 38)*

◆ *Wok-Fried Hokkien Noodles with Black Beans, Asian Greens & Shiitake Mushrooms (p. 44)*

◆ *Asian Greens with Shiitake Mushrooms & Black Bean Sauce (p. 46)*

◆ *Malaysian Mushroom Curry (p. 48)*

◆ *Tom Kha Hed (p. 56)*

Rosalind Carrarini

VILLANDRY

◆ *Paris Mushroom, Fennel & Parmesan Salad (p. 104)*

◆ *Giant Portobello Mushrooms with Artichoke Stew (p. 106)*

◆ *Paris Mushrooms with Egg Strips & Soy Sauce (p. 138)*

David Chia, Graham Harris,

Adrian McCormack

WAGAMAMA

◆ *Zasai Gohan (p. 22)*

◆ *Yasai Chili Men (p. 29)*

◆ *Moyashi Soba (p. 54)*

Chris Kwan

ZEN CENTRAL

◆ *Chinese Mushrooms Stir-fried with Chicken Fillet in Sichuan Hot Sauce (p. 24)*

◆ *Crispy Button Mushrooms with Peppercorn, Salt & Chili (p. 32)*

◆ *Oyster Mushrooms in Black Bean Sauce (p. 36)*

index

acknowledgments

The publishers would like to thank all the chefs who kindly contributed their time and talents to the book – in particular Daniel del Vecchio and Shaun Gilmore, Chris Benians, Mark Gregory and Cyrus Todiwala. Special thanks also to Mike Spiller, Lesley Levine, Dorothy Groves, Kerri Pritchard, Tanya Webb, Suzanna Obank, Amanda Leung, Yasemin Olcay, and Edouard Hempel at Wild Harvest.

Color Reproduction by Global Color

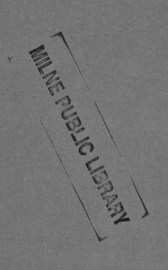